I CHOOSE LOVE

HOW TO LOVE YOUR NEIGHBOR AS YOURSELF

CHIP INGRAM

MOODY PUBLISHERS
CHICAGO

Some names and details have been changed to protect the privacy of individuals.

Edited by Cheryl Dunlop Molin
Interior design: Kaylee Lockenour Dunn and Tammy Adelhardt
Cover design and artwork: Thom Hoyman

For more resources, go to www.LivingontheEdge.org.

ISBN: 978-0-8024-3789-1

Originally delivered by fleets of horse-drawn wagons, the affordable paperbacks from D. L. Moody's publishing house resourced the church and served everyday people. Now, after more than 125 years of publishing and ministry, Moody Publishers' mission remains the same—even if our delivery systems have changed a bit. For more information on other books (and resources) created from a biblical perspective, go to www.moodypublishers.com or write to:

Moody Publishers
820 N. LaSalle Boulevard
Chicago, IL 60610

1 3 5 7 9 10 8 6 4 2

Printed in the United States of America

Praise for *I Choose Love*

Chip Ingram has often urged Christians to "bring light instead of heat" to a hostile culture. In this book, he reminds us that the early church grew by prioritizing agape love, demonstrated through humility, availability, intentionality, and self-sacrifice. Using his powerful, practical suggestions, readers will be inspired and equipped to do likewise, here and now.

Jim Daly, President, *Focus on the Family*

We live in a world that talks endlessly about love but seems to have no idea what it actually is. Chip Ingram cuts through the noise with biblical clarity and practical wisdom. *I Choose Love* doesn't offer easy answers or feel-good platitudes—it presents the radical, costly, countercultural love of Christ that our relationships desperately need. This book will mess you up in the best possible way.

Kyle Idleman, Teaching Minister at Southeast Christian Church and author of *Not a Fan*

Chip Ingram is a trusted, steady voice in a day of confusion and compromise. I've had the privilege of interviewing Chip over the years and have marveled at the way he's navigated difficult topics with humility, love, and a redemptive perspective. He's exactly the one to write this book. He's been walking it out for many years. In a day of division, we need a deeper understanding of biblical love. We need to choose love so the world can heal and so that many will look up and trust God with their own stories. Take your time working through these pages. They'll change you from the inside out.

Susie Larson, Author, Radio Host, Speaker

I know of no author who better helps me to understand God and His love for me. Once again, God has used Chip to bring out a beautiful simplicity on the other side of theological complexity. We all need God's love, and this book helps us to better understand, receive, and then pass it along for God's glory and our joy.

Henry Kaestner, cofounder, Faith Driven Entrepreneur, Faith Driven Investor

To the one who wants to choose a life of love and live a Christ-centered, others-focused life, this book is for you. Chip Ingram is one of my favorite authors because he writes exceptional books that are transforming. *I Choose Love* just may be his best.

Jack Graham, Senior Pastor, Prestonwood Baptist Church, Plano, TX

Could there be a better prepared or more reliable guide to helping believers reach their neighbors for Christ than Chip Ingram? I cannot think of one. In *I Choose Love,* Chip leads us to remember that we are loved—and then challenges us to do likewise. Read this book and be prepared to choose love.

Mark Yarbrough, President, Dallas Theological Seminary; author of *The Rekindled Heart*

Chip Ingram is one of my favorite Bible teachers! As I read this book, I realized that choosing love is a "learned trait." Some of us grew up not either fully understanding how to choose the right kind of love or we drifted along the way. Chip unpacks love from a biblical understanding that is profound, life-changing, and simple, but not always easy. There are amazing insights on every page.

Jim Burns, PhD, founder, HomeWord; author of *Doing Life with Your Adult Children: Keep Your Mouth Shut and the Welcome Mat Out*

In the struggle to represent Christ with both grace and truth, I've found no better Bible teacher than Chip Ingram to faithfully apply God's Word to my life and relationships. Jesus told us the definitive trait of His followers is our "love one for another." How can you love like this in a world of division and hostility? What does it look like today? Chip's new book, *I Choose Love*, equips you to follow Jesus in today's divisive culture. This in-depth Bible study is practical, inspiring, and maturing.

John S. Dickerson, Lead Pastor, Connection Pointe Christian Church, and author of *Jesus Skeptic*

I dedicate this book to Dave Marshall, Glen Miller, Bill Carter, Howard Hendricks, Bill Lawrence, Don Geiger, A.C. Musgrave, and Dick Sleeper – my mentors by life and word who have loved me deeply.

If you're a pastor and plan to teach the principles in this book, you can **download Chip Ingram's free teaching notes** from Moody Publishers by visiting online or scanning the QR code.

MOODYPUBLISHERS.COM/I-CHOOSE-LOVE

Contents

Introduction

Love is the most talked about and written about topic in the history of the world.

We all long to be loved. From the moment we are born to the moment we die, placed within each human heart is a passionate desire to be cared for, to belong, to be valued, to be cherished, and to be connected with other human beings. We want to be valued just for who we are.

As I thought about this common desire in all of us, I did a little informal research on the internet. Did you know according to ChatGPT that there are more than 100 million love songs already written, and that the first one discovered goes all the way back to 2000 BC in Mesopotamia in the library of Ashurbanipal?

I was also struck at the sheer volume of the use of the word *love* in songs of all kinds. It is the most common word used in any song that has ever been written. In fact, songs about finding love, losing love, or promising to keep love are the most common by far. Of the top 100 love songs of all time, the following titles reveal our desire, frustration, and heartaches that come from our search to be loved:

"My Girl" by The Temptations
"I Will Always Love You" by Whitney Houston
"How Deep Is Your Love" by the Bee Gees
"Eternal Flame" by the Bangles
"Endless Love" by Lionel Richie

"Can't Help Falling in Love" by Elvis Presley
"All of Me" by John Legend
"Best of My Love" by The Eagles and The Emotions
"Love Me Tender" by Elvis Presley
"I Love You Always Forever" by Donna Lewis

The most streamed song of all time, "Blinding Lights," with 4.89 billion streams as of this writing, is about love that could have been, but was lost. Most of us have been there at one time or another and can identify with that pain. But music isn't the only place where love is the hottest topic. You may not be surprised to learn that 33 percent of all mass-market paperback books are in the romance genre. And in like manner, the hottest Google searches in 2024 revolved around insights into our love lives. Everything from dating apps to losing love, from keeping love to knowing if you are in love, and of course, defining love.

A ChatGPT search about love and relationships revealed "about 62 percent of men are sure that they are in love with their partner compared to 57 percent of women who report the same. In a strange but common dynamic, revealing the elusiveness of love—38 percent of women have thought about leaving their partners while 29 percent of men thought of doing the same." I don't present this as empirical evidence, but simply to point out the preoccupation and fickleness of "love" as it is in today's culture.

Maybe that's why the greatest love song of all time (remaining number one on the top 100 pop charts for fourteen straight weeks in 1992) was "I Will Always Love You" sung by Whitney Houston.

What's most revealing about the more modern expressions of love is that they have mostly to do with romantic and erotic love. They have to do with finding that special person, or losing that special person, or the pain of never having had that special person.

I share this not to trivialize this desire by any means, but to emphasize the fact that we were made for relationship, and that we all long to be loved. It's clear from the volume about this topic, whether in songs or books or poetry or streaming content or television and movies, that we human beings have a deep desire to be accepted, to belong, to be safe, to be valued, and to be the object of someone else's affection, just for who we are.

In more recent times, and especially in popular culture, love has been redefined almost exclusively around the romantic and erotic. This has not been the case historically or linguistically. In today's world "love" expresses a journey of peaks and valleys, a never-ending search, realization and loss for that transcendent romantic feeling and/or sexual expression that validates "I am loved, I belong, I am valued, I have permanency and meaning because of this relationship."

What most of the songs, books, and media about love have in common is the idea that this elusive, deeply sought experience and connection with another person will somehow, some way, in some semi-magical manner come into my life as I wait for that right person or right moment of destiny.

Love is viewed primarily as something that happens to me and for which I have great desire, but little control.

This book will challenge the above premise at its core. The title alone screams that love is far from being something that might happen someday, some way, if everything goes your way . . . but instead, it's something you actually can *choose* to experience.

Now to be fair, this confusing and complex word we call *love* needs to be identified, defined, and parsed if we're to ever understand it, let alone experience it. As we all know, the word *love* has a wide variety of meanings in English. We can say with all sincerity that we love pizza, we love a sports team, we love how someone is dressed, we love our spouse or children, and we love God. We know intuitively that it's not the same kind of love and yet, in English, we use the same word.

The Greek language in which the New Testament was written is far more precise. There are at least four separate words used for love, and they all have a very definitive meaning. They also have significant implications in how they relate to one another. (For a fuller treatment of the four kinds of love I highly recommend C. S. Lewis's book by that title.)

This book is about choosing love, not any kind of love, but a love that the Bible calls *agape* love. It's the kind of love God has for people, which is characterized primarily not by our feelings or emotions, but by sacrifice and whatever puts others' best interests at heart. It's not emotionless, it's not some sterile or stoic response; but it's also not built on feelings, romantic notions, or erotic expectations. The diagram on the next page is a quick overview of the various kinds of love with a quick definition that will help you differentiate between God's love, a family's love, a friendship love, and a romantic, sensual kind of love. God created all four kinds of love and has given us clear instruction and commands concerning each kind of love so that we might flourish in every relationship in life.

The foundation is titled Agape Love (sacrificial, other-centered, spiritually empowered love); the next from the bottom would be Storgea Love (family love characterized by loyalty, devotion, and sacrifice around bloodlines or adoption); the third level would be Phileo Love (friendship, connection, personality, common cause, mutual benefit, and encouragement). At the top of the pyramid would be Eros Love (sexual and romantic love between a man and a woman in marriage). Marital love is built upon agape, storge, and phileo love and culminates in the gift of knowing and being known at the most intimate level in what the Bible describes as being naked and unashamed (Gen. 2:24–25). Paul defines the marriage relationship in Ephesians 5:22–23 as a holy picture and model of Jesus and His bride, the church. Marital love ideally results in the reproduction of life, and is intended for mutual pleasure and relational connection—solving the "aloneness" problem in Genesis 2. This special union is designed by God to be a physical and experiential oneness reflecting the deep sense of acceptance and belonging to know and to be known fully just for who we are. The marital eros love is differentiated from lust (see illustration below) as the goal even in sexual acts is to bring joy and fulfillment to one's partner, not focused on oneself. This other-centered, sacrificial giving, even in the romantic and sexual expressions of marriage, redefines love from God's perspective. The marriage bed is even described as "held in honor" in Scripture (Heb. 13:4).

FOR AN IN-DEPTH DEVELOPMENT SEE *THE FOUR LOVES* BY C. S. LEWIS.

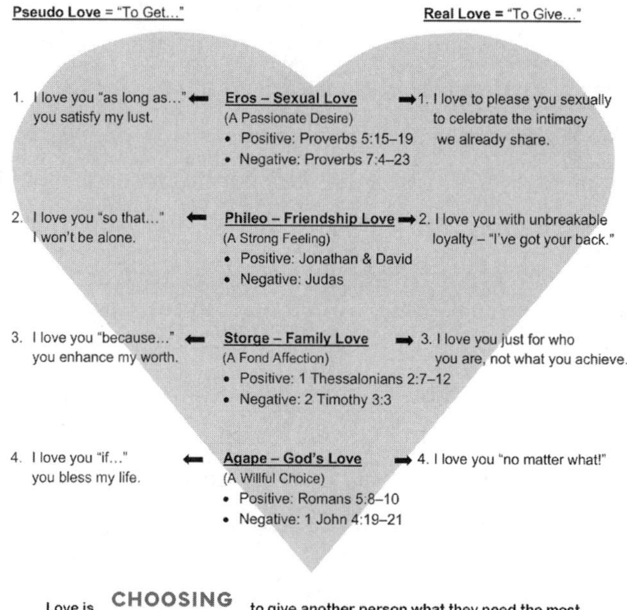

Looking at the illustration, you'll notice the foundation of all the other loves is this supernatural love that God has for us. It's a love He imparts to us and in us in order that we might love others as He has loved us. Agape love is giving another person what they need the most, when they deserve it the least, at great personal cost.

I realized from our time in marriage counseling that I couldn't give love that I did not have, and I could not change my spouse. But I could give her agape love as God has given to me, and that began a transformation in our marriage relationship. We both chose, regardless of how we felt, regardless of the hurts inflicted in the past on each other, to love the way God has loved us. That foundation, the loyalty of storgea love, and the joy and friendship of phileo love, led to a revitalized and fulfilling romantic eros love in our relationship.

If you long to be loved and to experience the love of God; if you long to learn to love others when you feel like it, and especially when you don't; if you long to get practical help to discover and apply agape love and see it transform all the other types of love, then this book is for you.

Its content comes from an unlikely context to learn about love. It's an exposition of a letter the apostle Paul wrote to a church that he dearly loved in the city of Philippi. They were experiencing some significant external pressure from their culture and some internal conflict in the church that caused him to write this thank-you letter for their ministry to him. These Holy Spirit–inspired words about how they could learn to love one another as they followed the example and teaching of Jesus are revolutionary.

I've pastored now for about forty years and have engaged in hundreds if not thousands of counseling conversations. I've had a front-row seat to many sad endings and some beautiful reconciliations. I've talked with lifelong friends who let politics or a doctrinal issue ruin their relationships. I've met with scores of couples who had lost all emotional connection with one another and were living separate lives and headed for divorce prior to discovering the power of agape love. I've listened to the frustrations and pain from single adults whose longings and dreams have been unrealized and who were in despair prior to grasping and experiencing God's agape love. I've met with countless family members who've hurt one another over the years, had ongoing miscommunication and misunderstandings that created hostility and pain, until at least one party realized they could *choose* love and see God begin to work.

Learning to receive and practice agape love is the key to every relationship.

Many chose not to and they live with bitterness and regret; but many learned what we will discover together in this book—how to choose love and then experience it. Regardless of where your joys or struggles reside when you look at that "Four Kinds of Love" graphic, I guarantee that learning to receive and practice agape love is the key to every relationship. And the good news is it's not something you have to wait for; it's available now, and in abundance and with God's promise that "love never fails" (1 Cor. 13:8).

As you scanned the table of contents, I'm sure you noticed that God's kind of love is characterized by four very important words: love *gives, serves, obeys,* and *cares.*

Together we will learn the counterintuitive and supernatural nature of love, which grows and multiplies, not by getting what we want all the time, but by choosing to *give,* and trusting how God works in us and for us and through us in ways that no amount of *getting* can ever achieve.

We'll discover the amazing power of *serving* and the joy that comes when our focus is off of ourselves and our needs and onto the needs of others. We will learn that God loves to exalt and lift up those who serve and do for them beyond what they ever dreamed or could ever acquire on their own.

We'll face the harsh reality that to *obey* when we don't feel like it is hard, and it feels impossible. We'll learn that our feelings don't have mastery over us and that when we choose to obey, especially when we don't feel like it, amazing things happen first *in* us and then *through* us. We will learn that God doesn't evaluate our love for Him by our intentions or emotions, but it is when we obey His Word that we demonstrate our love for Him (John 14:21).

Finally, we will experience the relational revolution that occurs when we develop the practice of simply *caring* about those around us. In small ways and in big ways we will learn that a caring smile, a caring act, and a caring word open doors, break down walls, and connect people to one another's hearts.

> When we choose to obey, especially when we don't feel like it, amazing things happen first *in* us and then *through* us.

I have imperfectly learned to give, serve, obey, and care; especially when I haven't felt like it. This book will teach you not only what God says, but will help you put it into practice in such a way that you can "choose love" in every relationship and in every situation. Perfectly, of course not; significantly with life-transforming impact, absolutely!

So, I challenge you to break free of that victim mentality that waits for love to happen to you; and declare to God, to yourself, and especially to those close to you that you will *choose* love.

Part 1: Love Gives

For God so loved the world that he *gave* his one and only Son, that whoever believes in him shall not perish but have eternal life.

John 3:16 NIV

Chapter 1

Love Gives

One of the most obvious results of being loved is that it makes us happy. It brings us joy. That's how God made it to work. Jesus' final words about His love for His disciples and why He was willing to lay down His life for them (and us) are summarized in John 15:11: "These things I have spoken to you so that My joy may be in you, and that your joy may be made full."

Did you know you can actually make God happy? To many people, that's a strange thought—that the unchanging, invisible, infinite Creator who has no beginning or end, who is all-powerful and all-knowing, who is awesome in majesty and glory, existing outside of time and space, can experience joy even from one person out of the billions who live on this tiny planet in His universe.

An impersonal force wouldn't get pleasure from a little finite human being, but God is not an impersonal force. He's a person. He is relational and has thoughts and feelings about His relationships. And every human being, including you, has the potential to bring joy to His heart.

One of God's greatest joys is when His children love each other.

If you're a parent, you can probably understand why. Theresa and I have four children, and our oldest are fraternal twins, Eric and Jason. When they were young, they slept in the same room, wore matching clothes, had the same haircuts, and shared many of the same friends. As they grew older, they shared a lot of the same experiences. They also fought. A lot. They teased and provoked each other. Jason was bigger than Eric, so he tried to make his brother do all kinds of things he didn't want to do himself. They lived in a constant state of tension.

Once when Theresa and I went away for a weekend, the boys especially got under each other's skin, and not surprisingly, they ended up in a fight. At some point in all the wrestling and pushing, one of them put a fist or an elbow through the wall, and they did a pretty good job of patching it up. When we returned, they acted as if nothing had happened, although we did wonder why they were standing against a wall in an awkward position. It wasn't until they were grown that they finally confessed. They were kind of shocked that we never even noticed the damage.

Theresa grew up with two sisters. So did I. We weren't quite sure what to make of all the fighting. I remember Theresa asking me once if I thought they would ever love each other, and I tried to reassure her.

"Of course, honey," I said, trying to sound convinced. "This is normal at their age."

"Normal?" she said. "They're in the next room arguing and wrestling on the floor!"

They eventually grew out of it, but the thought of them having a loving relationship with each other still seemed like a stretch. But when Jason was a young adult and was preparing to move to Nashville to pursue a career in music, he performed a concert at our church. One of the songs he sang that night was a song he had written to Eric about how much he loved him. Theresa and I sat on the front row, bawling. To this day, they are best friends, and all those years of wondering if they would ever stop trying to hurt each other are a distant memory.

Few things stress parents out more than their children fighting each other, and few things bring greater joy to parents than their children loving each other. And since God is the ultimate Father who even defines Himself by His love, we can be certain that He gets a lot of joy when His people love each other too.

We live in a world that seems more divided than ever, and in many ways, the church is nearly as divided as the world. We may strive for unity, and we may even hold it as one of our highest ideals (though some don't seem to care about it very much), but no one has been very successful at resolving divisions in the world or the church. And for the church, a people who are called to represent the nature of God and live on earth as the body of Christ, that's a problem.

In fact, it's more than a problem. It's a crisis. Few things rob us of our joy like disunity; and few things discredit our testimony to the world like disunity. Unless Christians are able to live in love and unity, the world has every right to say, "I don't believe in your Jesus." There's a lot at stake.

A PRAYER THAT ONLY YOU CAN ANSWER

> One of God's greatest joys is to see
> His children love each other.

The night before Jesus was crucified, He prayed a sweeping, profound prayer that expressed His greatest desires for His followers.

We get to eavesdrop on that prayer in John's gospel, and Jesus begins with a summary of His ministry and how He has fulfilled it. He then asks the Father to protect and preserve the faith of His followers in this hostile world. But the climax of the prayer is His request for the three-way relationship between His followers, Himself, and the Father: "That they may be one, just as We are one. I in them and You in Me, that they may be perfected in unity, so that the world may know that You sent Me, and loved them, even as You have loved Me" (John 17:22–23). In other words, that believers would be united with Jesus and each other in the same way that Jesus and the Father are united.

Unity. Loving each other. Demonstrating the love of God as evidence to the world that Jesus is real.

That's a prayer only we can answer.

It's an amazing prayer, and if we look just at the surface, we might wonder if it will ever be answered. Across the board, believers do not appear to be united on much of anything, even within the same denominations and churches. The spiritual reality in Jesus' prayer is that Christians around the world already are united with Jesus and each other. True believers are family, born of the same Spirit. But demonstrating that unity is another matter.

You play a part in answering that prayer—in your family, at work, in your community, at church, everywhere. Every one of us is called to embody the love and unity of the Father, Son, and Holy Spirit in our relationships with Him and other believers. And even though we are commanded to be separate from the world, we are called to express the love of God that flows from our union with Him.

This is not just a "wouldn't it be nice" kind of ideal. It's imperative. This is where we most clearly reflect the heart of God. If we aren't living in that kind of unity, we aren't reflecting His nature.

In Philippians 2, the foundational biblical text for the message of this book, the apostle Paul is going to command what Jesus has prayed. But before we get into that passage, I want to be clear about our purpose. The point is not just to understand these words academically—the original context, sentence structure, and intended meaning—but to radically reframe our relationships. Nearly all of us have people in our life who rub us the wrong way, always seem to disagree, or even make us question our own sanity. For you, it may be someone in your own home, another family member, a coworker, or people at church who don't share your vision for how things ought to be or seem to love playing the role of antagonist whenever new ideas come up. You wish certain people were nicer, more agreeable, more generous, less angry . . . anything other than what they are.

Nothing will change until we bring our relationships before God and listen to what He is saying about them.

Which of your relationships is affected by unresolved (and perhaps even unresolvable) conflict? Which ones prompt feelings of bitterness, anger, frustration, or regret? Which seem impossible to navigate because of differing values, personalities, or agendas? Who in your life do you wish you didn't have to deal with?

Whatever or whoever comes to mind when you think of these questions, let those relationships become the context for what God is speaking to you through His Word. Ask the Holy Spirit what He would have you address in them. Nothing will change until we bring our relationships before God and listen to what He is saying about them—and until we realize that unity begins with us. We will never experience the love and joy God wants for us until we honestly look at the "planks" in our eyes before we remove the "speck" in theirs.

If you have any relationships that keep going around in circles or repeatedly bring up an unhealthy response, you'll find Paul's words in this chapter to be revolutionary. They won't fix other people for you, and they won't cause everyone to agree on everything, but they will anchor your heart in the right place. It may not be easy or feel comfortable, but this is God's key to overcoming relational challenges and establishing the love and unity Jesus prayed for.

We'll explore what real unity means (and what it doesn't) later, but we need to know up front that many of the divisions we allow among us are breaking God's heart. When believers argue about our preferred political persuasion, the latest government policies, complex social issues that are difficult to interpret biblically, which channels and websites they are getting their news from, or even the style of church music or service formats—and judge people harshly for their position on these issues—we are not expressing God's heart.

Many of the divisions we allow among us are breaking God's heart.

We should talk about these things—they are important discussions to have—but they should never erode our fellowship. Genuine believers who love God deeply may come to very different conclusions on the issues we feel strongly about. When we do not demonstrate that we are bound together in love, even when we have different opinions, we undermine the gospel message of Jesus coming to earth to die on our behalf, raise us with Him to everlasting life, and build His church.

PAUL COMMANDS WHAT JESUS PRAYED

In his letter to the Philippians, Paul is addressing a church he loves. Of all the churches he founded and instructed, this was perhaps his most positive experience that we know about.

When Paul first went to Philippi, he didn't even find enough Jews to make up a synagogue, so he couldn't follow his normal pattern of preaching the gospel first to Jews, the most likely audience to accept his message. But there were some Jews and some God-fearers there—non-Jews who worshiped and honored the God of Israel without formally converting to Judaism. Paul found them by a river where they had gathered to pray.

There Paul met a woman named Lydia, who opened her heart to the gospel and welcomed Paul and his coworkers into her home. His ministry in Philippi came to a head when he and Silas were jailed and then miraculously delivered. A young slave girl who had a spirit of divination followed Paul and Silas around and kept shouting that they were servants of God proclaiming a way of salvation—a partial truth proclaimed in the wrong spirit—until Paul commanded the spirit to come out of her. Her owners, who profited from her fortune-telling, were angry and stirred up a crowd and the authorities against Paul and Silas. Paul and Silas then spent the night at the Philippian jail after being brutally beaten. In great pain and bound by shackles, they were worshiping God loudly when an earthquake broke them free. A terrified jailer and his household accepted Christ, Paul encouraged the young church that developed in his short time there, and then he departed the city.

The members of that church became some of Paul's most faithful supporters throughout his later ministry. When Paul was imprisoned in Rome and awaiting trial, they sent Epaphroditus, one of their members, with a financial gift because they knew prisoners had

> Authentic Christianity was just as unpopular then as it is now.

to pay for their own room and board. Epaphroditus encouraged Paul with news from the Philippian church, but he also shared some of the challenges they were facing. Paul's letter is his response to them. He thanks them for their generous gift; encourages them to face their challenges with faith, perseverance, and joy; and instructs them in how to resolve some of their difficulties. The result is one of the New Testament's most practically encouraging and edifying letters.

At the end of the first chapter, Paul reminds these believers, a small minority in a city that often opposed their faith, to endure. "For to you it has been granted for Christ's sake, not only to believe in Him, but also to suffer for His sake, experiencing the same conflict which you saw in me, and now hear to be in me" (Phil. 1:29–30). Authentic Christianity was just as unpopular then as it is now—countercultural movements always swim against the stream, and citizens of heaven living in a hostile world are as countercultural as you can get—and many believers were struggling. Some were intimidated, and their relationship with the pagan world around them was often contentious. Like many Christians today, as the world seeks to intimidate and silence followers of Jesus, many were growing more afraid to stand up and stand strong.

Those were the external pressures this church was facing, but they were also experiencing some internal pressures—specifically with two prominent women who were at odds with each other, and since Paul addresses them by name and requests outside help, it's likely creating a rift in the fellowship. Both of these women loved God and had been effectively used by Him, but they didn't get along. Paul addresses them specifically in Philippians 4, but their conflict is clearly in the background of chapter 2. As so often happens in churches, people tend to gravitate toward one side or the other when there's a conflict, and divisions develop. Many Philippian believers took sides. So Paul emphasized unity—authentic, Christ-empowered unity—in his letter.

That isn't the letter's only theme, or even its primary one. In the first chapter, he wrote about overcoming circumstances and having joy even in the midst of adversity. In chapters 3 and 4, he will write about how to embrace thoughts, perspectives, and priorities to live with peace and hope. All of these themes are woven throughout the letter.

But here in chapter 2, the primary emphasis is on unity, and according to Paul, there's only one way to achieve it: *Choose love.* And not just any love, as the world defines it, but God's kind of love (agape) that can radically change our own lives and the people around us.

The chapter begins with these profound words:

> Therefore if there is any encouragement in Christ, if there is any consolation of love, if there is any fellowship of the Spirit, if any affection and compassion, make my joy complete by being of the same mind, maintaining the same love, united in spirit, intent on one purpose. (Phil. 2:1–2)

On the surface, this may seem like just a nice thought, a pat on the back to encourage people to be kind to each other. But as we will see, Paul is getting to the heart of the gospel. He will even base these words on the incarnation—Jesus coming to earth in the form of a man in order to love, serve, and save us from this broken world. Choosing love makes us a lot like Him.

Choosing love makes us a lot like Him.

THE BIG IFS

The context of Paul's words in this chapter is this beloved church's relationship with the world and within their fellowship. They are experiencing external pressure from a community that rejects their faith and internal pressure from a growing conflict between two women and the people who have chosen sides, as well as confronting some false teachings. The first chapter ended with some instructions about how to navigate their world and the pressures society was placing on them. Here in chapter 2, Paul addresses their internal relationships with each other. He wants them to live in authentic, Christ-empowered unity.

This unity is important to Paul. It will "make [his] joy complete." Like God and loving parents, Paul will get pleasure from seeing his loved ones genuinely get along. Authentic, Christ-empowered unity doesn't just mean putting up with each other or having a superficial peace. It's from the heart.

To make his case, Paul begins with a series of "ifs," all leading up to a "then." *If* you have any encouragement, *if* any comfort, *if* any fellowship with the Spirit, *if* any tenderness and compassion . . . *then* make my joy complete. How? By being of the same mind, having the same love, being united in spirit and purpose.

Nearly every religion has some version of the Golden Rule—"Do unto others as you would have them do unto you." Jesus preached it in the Sermon on the Mount (see Matt. 7:12), and Paul presents it here. But Paul, inspired by the Holy Spirit, goes even further with it. Other religions may copy the "Golden Rule," but here God calls us to the "Platinum Rule." Here we are commanded, "Do unto others as God has already done unto you." Love and unity flourish when we base our love not on what we would like others to do for us, but when we base it on what Jesus has already done for us. Paul's message is, "I want you to love other people the way Christ has loved you."

We tend to think our relational conflicts and struggles are only horizontal, person-to-person issues. When we say things like, "Look at what she did," or, "He doesn't deserve that," or "Only when she apologizes," we're thinking horizontally. We're forgetting all the ways God has shown us mercy, given us grace, and demonstrated His vast, magnanimous love for us. Our basis for loving people doesn't depend on how they have treated us. It depends on how *God* has treated us. The way we respond to them is a choice based on His love. We choose to love like He does.

Our basis for loving people doesn't depend on how they have treated us. It depends on how *God* has treated us.

The Platinum Rule

Do unto others as God has already done unto you.

So Paul reminds the Philippians of the love they have been given. All of his "ifs" in this passage seem to convey the message that things are still up in the air—that his instructions are conditional, depending on whether the Philippians are really experiencing this kind of encouragement, comfort, fellowship, and tender compassion. That's how we understand "if" in English. But the Greek word "if" in this passage is a grammatical construction that carries a broader meaning "since" or "because." Paul is essentially saying, "*Because* you have this encouragement, comfort, fellowship, and tender compassion, *then* love and unity should be the natural outcome."

Since or *because* we have experienced something of God's nature deep inside our hearts through being born of His Spirit and having an intimate relationship with Him, then love and unity are the result. Every time we are hurting and struggling, we can connect with God's heart and know that He cares. Through fellowship with Him, we experience His encouragement, comfort, and compassion, and therefore we are called to share the same with others.

The word "tenderness" here refers to our deep, inward parts—literally our bowels, the place where visceral emotions were thought to be located, akin to our use of the word *heart*. The tenderness of God's character is imbedded deep within us, assuring us that we are His treasure, His delight. "Compassion" here refers to an outward expression of that tenderness. It's the evidence of what God has done and is doing within us. Because His compassion always leads to action—notice how many times in the Gospels Jesus had compassion on the multitudes and began healing and restoring their lives—our compassion should always lead to action too.

If I were to rephrase what Paul is saying, I'd put it like this: "God has put His arm around you in Jesus, put His Spirit within you, and is walking with you through this new life. He has given you comfort in your hurts and struggles in this difficult and challenging world; you are now a temple of the Holy Spirit and have a growing level of intimacy with Him as you walk with Him; and you have a tender compassion that grows out of God's tender compassion in loving, forgiving, and restoring you. Because of all that, here's how you need to respond." And then Paul gives us four ways to respond to what God has done for us in Christ.

1. Be of the same mind. This phrase in Greek literally means "think the same thing," and Paul's focus here is on truth. It would be a mistake to think that if we feel right about each other and come together in unity, truth no longer matters—that our understanding of the Bible and beliefs about morality are relative or irrelevant or somehow pushed to the side. There are people who believe that none of that matters as long as we are at peace with each other. But that isn't true at all. Paul is saying just the opposite. Genuine unity demands truth. We can love people with a different understanding of what the Bible teaches, but we can't afford to compromise truth in order to have peace. Peace at any price isn't real peace.

We live in a world that doesn't grasp this principle and often even opposes the very idea of truth. It is common now for people to talk about "my truth" and "your truth," as though truth were in the eye of the beholder, and any challenge to what someone holds to be true would be met with blowback. Though standing up for truth is actually a loving response to a misguided society, it is considered politically incorrect to reject someone's version of truth, no matter how distorted it is. Some even call this defense of truth "hate."

Standing up for truth is actually a loving response to a misguided society.

Unfortunately but understandably, many Christians have been affected by the boundaries the world has placed on us. We've let secular values intimidate us into silence. Many Christians are very hesitant to publicly oppose popular opinions and have learned to keep quiet about their convictions because they know the reaction they would get. They would be seen as ignorant or hateful.

Sadly, we have also carried our sense of intimidation and desire to be politically correct with us into the church. Instead of directly addressing untruths among other believers, we often wait until we get home to talk about all the things people get wrong. We make truth a private matter rather than a fellowship issue. Of course, I'm not suggesting we should be argumentative, accusing, or unloving in any way. I am suggesting, however, that both in the world and among other believers, we need to do a better job of speaking the truth in love (Eph. 4:15).

Here's an example of how to respond to a fellow believer's inaccurate or doctrinally false comment: "I know that's a popular thought, but can you tell me where it's found in Scripture? I really want to understand where you're coming from, but I also want to make sure we're basing our beliefs on what God says and not what the world says or what feels right to us. What did Jesus say about this issue? What does God reveal in the Bible about it?"

Far from being a legalistic straitjacket, His commands are given for our good.

That's a healthy conversation. The core issues we face in our society today are not primarily about gender dysphoria, race theory, political bias, a dysfunctional government, or any other topical point of contention. The real issue is whether absolute truth exists. Is there an unchanging reality? Who is the ultimate authority? For those of us who take the Bible seriously, God's revelation of truth defines what is right, moral, relationally appropriate, and healthy for us individually and as a society. Far from being a legalistic straitjacket, His commands are given for our good. The all-knowing, all-loving God who knows every detail of our lives—past, present, and future—gives us some parameters and prohibitions that will make it possible for us to flourish.

God wants us to have great relationships—satisfying marriages, healthy parenting, deep friendships, productive workplaces, strong communities, and flourishing churches. He gives us wise counsel regarding our finances, businesses, trials and adversity, and everything else we need to prosper spiritually, emotionally, relationally, and even materially. He tells us that those who delight in him are like trees planted by streams of water that yield their fruit in season, never withering and always prospering (Ps. 1). Those who heed His Word and avoid the counsel of the wicked are blessed (Ps. 1:1). Those who build their lives on the words of Jesus will stand strong forever (Matt. 7:24–27). God's truth, even when it seems difficult, is all for our good.

That's worth standing up for, even when people misunderstand us and think we're being narrow-minded. The fellowship of believers depends on truth tellers because truth is necessary for love and unity. But we need to present it gently, winsomely, and without accusation or anger.

2. *Maintain the same love.* Paul urges us to mutually love one another the way God has loved us—honestly and sacrificially. In another letter, where Paul defines what it means to be a disciple of Jesus, he describes what love looks like in the body of Christ: "Let love be without hypocrisy. Abhor what is evil; cling to what is good. Be devoted to one another in brotherly love" (Rom. 12:9–10). He goes on in that passage to talk about honoring each other, being diligent and fervent as we serve the Lord together, contributing to each other's needs, rejoicing in hope, persevering in tribulation (vv. 9–13). This is sacrificial, other-centered love that says, "I've got your back. We're in this together. I care about you." This kind of love is built on truth and is filled with the kind of love Jesus modeled for His disciples.

3. *United in spirit.* A literal rendering of this word is "one in soul," or to be like-souled. In other words, we have a common heart. In our relationships, we're real, without duplicity, not superficial but deeply joined together in a common spirit for a common purpose.

When we're honest with ourselves, many of us have to admit we're just try to get by in our relationships. We don't want the intensity or burden of going deep and resolving issues. So we remain on the surface, maintaining a superficial peace while overlooking real conflict and unresolved issues. We don't want to rock the boat.

I grew up in a family where we all walked on eggshells around my father. He'd become a functioning alcoholic after trauma from WWII; any wrong word or action could set off an angry outburst. I learned to be less than honest, keep the peace, and avoid conflict at all costs; unfortunately, those patterns caused huge problems early in our marriage. I wasn't honest with how I really felt about some things with Theresa if I thought it would produce conflict. I buried hurt feelings and inwardly blamed her for things I never had the courage or the skills to share with her. It was only after some biblical marriage counseling that we both learned to speak the truth in love (Eph. 4:15). It changed a superficial, struggling marriage into an intimate one over time.

As iron sharpens iron, we sharpen each other, even though sharpening iron always produces some sparks.

That's *not* the kind of relationship Jesus had with His disciples or that Paul is talking about here. The bonds of love and unity go deep and cultivate intimacy. As iron sharpens iron, we sharpen each other, even though sharpening iron always produces some sparks.

I think most people are reluctant to go there because they see conflict as a problem. They believe it means something is wrong and therefore is something to avoid. But conflict may just mean that other people have a different perspective that comes from a different background, and if we're to challenge each other and learn from each other, it's important to explore those differences. Having a common heart does not mean having an identical heart.

We don't have to agree or prove who is right. But we do need to draw near to each other in love.

4. *Intent on one purpose.* What is that purpose? God gave us a command to love Him with all our heart, soul, mind, and strength, and Jesus affirmed this as the greatest commandment, along with loving our neighbors as ourselves. It's a purpose we can all agree on, regardless of our political, social, theological, denominational perspectives. We don't have to agree on all the issues confronting our society, but we do need to agree on loving God with everything in us, and on loving our neighbors as ourselves.

We also need to agree on going into all the world to disciple every nation. That's the Great Commission that follows the Great Commandment. And we could add a Great Compassion to that: to agree that when we've loved and served "the least of these" (Matt. 25:40, 45)—the suffering, weak, marginalized, oppressed people of this world—we've loved and served Jesus and represented who He is.

I have sought to obey and practice the Great Commandment, the Great Commission, and the Great Compassion with a lot of people who are on the other side of the aisle from where I sit. On many issues, we have not been on the same page at all. But we do agree on those essentials. Other issues that define our differences may be important, but these are so much more important. I have learned that I don't need to agree on secondary doctrines, political positions, or best practices to address controversial issues to have meaningful, deep, Christ-centered relationships. They last forever. So we come together in unity, in spite of our differences, to live for the same purpose with a common heart.

These four imperatives are a response to what God has done for us. What we have received from Him, we pass on to others. This is how we make God's (and Paul's) joy complete: by being of one mind in truth, caring for one another with one heart, connecting as one soul, and having a common purpose in advancing the gospel. These are specific, clear choices to make love (agape) the priority, not our preferences.

What does that look like? The thousands of different ministries that are being carried out in hundreds of thousands of churches and Christian organizations to love people, feed the poor, care for the sick, help those struggling with sin and personal issues without condemning or marginalizing them, and preaching the good news of redemption and restoration everywhere. That's the kind of love that turned the world upside down in the first century and continues to turn the world upside down today—person by person, family by family, church by church, and community by community.

A PORTRAIT OF LOVE

When we get to heaven, we will probably be shocked to discover what we were wrong about. We'll find out that we were right about a lot of things, but we'll also realize that we disagreed with some people who turned out to be right. No matter how well we think our minds reason, we don't have the full picture or flawless logic. When God reveals all of humanity's misunderstandings, none of us is going to come away with a perfect scorecard.

But even though Scripture doesn't resolve all of our political, social, theological, and methodological differences—or at least our imperfect understanding of Scripture does not—it does give us a clear picture of what love looks like. We can thank Paul for this description too; it's what he had in mind as he wrote to the Corinthians about loving each other well.

> Love is patient, love is kind and is not jealous; love does not brag and is not arrogant, does not act unbecomingly; it does not seek its own, is not provoked, does not take into account a wrong suffered, does not rejoice in unrighteousness, but rejoices with the truth; bears all things, believes all things, hopes all things, endures all things. Love never fails. (1 Cor. 13:4–8)

We live in a time when love is treated as a feeling. According to popular perception, if you have a good feeling about something, then any "truth," any behavior, any boundaries or lack thereof are fair game. After all, love is love, and it trumps everything else in life. And to love someone means to accept whatever they say and do as valid, because not to do so would be an attack on their identity. Love means anything goes.

But biblical love is not that blind, nor that shallow. It may involve emotions much of the time, but it is not ruled by them. It is a choice made with eyes wide open. It does not ignore truth. In fact, it fully embraces truth and rejoices in it. But it remains patient, kind, selfless, faithful, hopeful, and enduring.

To experience biblical love, we must realize that it doesn't just happen. It doesn't become a full and fruitful part of our lives passively. It isn't dependent on whims or moods or even on natural compatibility. Love is God's core attribute, planted within us by the Spirit who gives us life by grace through faith. God has already granted it to us, and it's up to us to live in it.

And the only way to do that is to *choose* it in every situation, with everyone.

QUESTIONS FOR REFLECTION/DISCUSSION

1. Why is our unity so important to God? Read John 13:34–35 for added insight.

2. What relationship is the most challenging in your life right now? Why?

3. What insight from this chapter might help you "do your part" in improving it?

4. What's the difference between the Golden Rule and the Platinum Rule? How does that change our common tendency to wait for the other person to change before we do?

5. What specific act of love do you sense God is directing you to choose this week?

CHAPTER 2

How to Become a More Loving Person

Imagine getting to heaven and seeing how often you were wrong about something—not necessarily in your beliefs, priorities, or plans for your life (though none of us is 100 percent accurate in all of that), but in some of the smaller issues like assumptions about other people, misunderstandings in a relationship, making decisions about your future, political perspectives, or conversations in which you powerfully and persuasively explained why you were right and the other person was dead wrong, only to discover it was really the other way around. Scripture is very clear about a lot of things, so we know our faith will be vindicated when we get there. But I have a sneaking suspicion we'll find out that our view of the world and other people wasn't always on target. It will be a humbling experience.

Now imagine bringing that future humility into your present experience. You do not yet know which of your perspectives are right or wrong, but you do know you'll have some of each. None of us is omniscient and we will never grasp things perfectly. What if that kind of awareness began to show up in your conversations? How might an extra dose of humility help you become a more loving person?

This is the direction Paul takes us in the next few verses of Philippians 2. Love is paramount in God's kingdom. Paul ranked it above faith, hope, and all the gifts of the Spirit (1 Cor. 13), and it is God's defining attribute (1 John 4:8, 16) and, as we've seen, His greatest commandment (Matt. 22:36–40)—and humility is necessary for love. We simply cannot love pridefully. How we think about ourselves and others determines whether we are able to love people well. So in verses 3 and 4, Paul gives us a pathway to learn how to love better.

How we think about ourselves and others determines whether we are able to love people well.

If learning to love God and others well has not been your highest priority, now is a good time to put it at the top of your list. Without love, everything we accomplish is worthless. Paul wrote that even the greatest spiritual works profit us nothing if we don't have love (1 Cor. 13:3). If love is not at the center of our lives, our lives are not going to go in the direction God intends. So before we continue, stop right now and ask God: "Lord, will You help me learn to love better? Will You help me cultivate love for You and others as the driving force of my life?" You don't even have to add, "if it's Your will," at the end of it. Love is at the heart of His nature, and He delights in filling His people with it.

In Philippians 2:3–4, Paul gives us a blueprint for loving well. He outlines three practical steps to reshaping our attitudes to love people.

DECLARE WAR ON SELFISHNESS

The first step is radical: Declare war on selfishness. The reason I'm putting this in such strong, aggressive terms is that our self-centeredness doesn't disappear with a mere suggestion or mild rebuke. It is relentless, so we need to be decisive and relentless in dealing with it.

This is why Paul begins with a very clear command: "Do nothing from selfishness or empty conceit, but with humility of mind regard one another as more important than yourselves" (Phil. 2:3). That doesn't leave much room for interpretation, does it? "Nothing" means nothing. Everything we do should be done in a spirit of humility.

A lot of people aren't aware that they have a problem with selfishness, perhaps because we tend to define it as being arrogant or self-absorbed. But even the most unassuming people can be self-focused. I think of selfishness not necessarily as being consumed with yourself all the time, but as best defined by four words: "I want my way."

Selfishness is a "me first" mindset. I want to be the first in line, get on the plane first, get to work first, go through the buffet line first, get the best promotion, prioritize my needs in this relationship, be number one in every situation, and on and on. It's easy to see this attitude in others as they cut in front of you on the highway or carry a winner-takes-all attitude into the workplace. But others have seen it in each of us too. All of us have demonstrated this ambitious, competitive, self-serving approach to life in a variety of ways, often without even recognizing it.

I have some grandchildren who are still pretty young, and as with every other child I've ever known, no one has had to teach them how to be selfish. Put any two kids in a room with one desirable snack or toy, and you'll see this at work. It's part of our nature from the beginning, and even if we mature and become more selfless over time, we never completely grow out of our "me first" mindset. We just get more sophisticated in expressing it.

There's only one antidote for that ugly, subtle, selfish core of our being: humility. You don't just slide out of selfishness casually. You can only get over it by radically and resolutely embracing humility. It's a hard-won battle because selfishness is deeply rooted in our hearts.

Humility is not about cutting yourself down a few notches or beating yourself up. It's simply having an accurate view of yourself—not too high, not too low. As has been wisely said, "Humility isn't thinking less of yourself. It's thinking of yourself less."

Humility is not about cutting yourself down a few notches or beating yourself up.

Recent research on humility is surprisingly encouraging. Psychologists have focused quite a few virtue studies on solving negative behaviors; you may be familiar with some on generosity, thankfulness, and various other traits that have made the news in recent years. We've learned that generous people have better relationships, more friends, lower blood pressure, and longer lives. We've learned that gratitude can radically change a person's well-being. Psychologists and social scientists are discovering that the wisdom in some of the shortest verses in the Bible—"Rejoice always; pray without ceasing; in everything give thanks; for this is God's will for you in Christ Jesus" (1 Thess. 5:16–18)—is profound, powerful, and life-changing.

A study on humility by a professor at George Fox University has likewise confirmed the power of humility. Researchers developed scales to measure intellectual humility, relational humility, and cultural humility, and some are also working on spiritual humility. They are finding that humble people have less anxiety about death, better romantic relationships, less spiritual struggle, better performance at school and work, more compassion for others, and greater self-esteem than those who are less humble. They are also more grateful and forgiving, so they enjoy the benefits of those virtues in addition to the benefits of humility.[1]

Amazing, right? Anyone want to talk about how "restrictive" and "narrow-minded" the Bible is now? Or maybe ancient revelation from the all-wise God is exactly what humanity needs for a flourishing life. When you live consistently with the way God has designed His world to work, you discover that His way works out well for you. And His way is usually counterintuitive to the ways selfish hearts and minds have chosen.

In this article, the researchers go on to define humility. It does not require self-loathing or self-belittling—that's not humility—but calls for us to dial back our normal tendency to overestimate our abilities and behaviors. (Unfortunately I can relate, and I suspect you can too.)

Scientists point to three primary qualities of humble people: They (1) have a reasonably accurate view of themselves, neither too high nor too low; (2) reverse our natural human tendency to view ourselves with great generosity and others with suspicion; and (3) are teachable and open to new things. People who are not humble have a relatively distorted view of themselves, view others with suspicion, and are confident in their own assumptions so that they gravitate toward evidence that confirms what they already believe.

Paul tells us to do nothing from selfishness or empty conceit but with humility of mind, regarding others as more important than ourselves. You won't be able to do that by resolving to be a little nicer to people. Self-centeredness is endemic to the human race, deep down at the root of our fallenness, a part of our flesh that needs to be crucified. No matter how many Bible verses we've learned, no matter how much image management we've been able to perform or how effectively we've put on a veneer of humility, no matter how strong our willpower is, the flesh still wages war against the spirit (Gal. 5:16–17). At our core, we still want to get what we want.

We have to declare war on selfishness.

God often gives us what we want—He's the giver of beautiful and wonderful gifts that we can richly enjoy (1 Tim. 6:17; James 1:17)—but He doesn't want us prioritizing those gifts in a way that shifts our focus to spending our lives looking out for ourselves. We are to relate to Him and others humbly and sacrificially and trust Him to supply all our needs.

So we have to declare war on selfishness. We have to anchor ourselves in ultimate reality: "Jesus died for me, and in light of His sacrifice, I refuse to live a life that is focused on myself. I will do unto others not only as I want them to do unto me, but also according to what Jesus has already done for me. Because His Spirit is living in me, I can trust Him and depend on His power as I become other-centered and filled with His love. In community with His people, I will go into training to allow His Word and His Spirit to give me a humble heart, eyes filled with compassion, and a desire to serve."

It takes faith to do that. That kind of humility cuts radically against our fallen nature. We instinctually fear that if we aren't looking out for ourselves, no one else will. But by faith, we know God will. And according to the promise of Jesus, whatever we give will be given to us in good measure—"pressed down, shaken together, and running over" (Luke 6:38). That's true not only financially (the context in which we often hear that verse), but even more in its original context of love and mercy.

This is ultimately not about how we conduct our relationships outwardly but about an inner attitude and mindset. When we seek to put others first, we will likely wonder, "What about me? Who's going to take care of my needs?" But Jesus promises that a supernatural principle of His kingdom is at work in whatever flows out of our lives. If we decide to be a great friend, we will receive great friends. If we choose to give our time to help other people, we will discover that other people give their time to help us. When we give generously of our talents and resources, we generally end up with more than we need. Whatever we pour out, He pours in, and usually in even greater measure (Matt. 6:33). This is not a "give to get" transactional mindset, but a Christlike model of putting others first in love.

That doesn't add up from a worldly point of view, but it does in God's economy. And because this is a supernatural kingdom principle that kicks in without any manipulation on our part, He gets credit for it. He is glorified in our selfless, humble reliance on Him.

ATTACK THE ROOT PROBLEM

The root of our problem is pride. That's the source of our selfishness. If we're going to embrace humility and love others well, we will need to do something about our own pride.

Pride is a big word. In verse 3, Paul calls it "empty conceit." Another translation says "vainglory" or vanity. It's that sometimes subtle sense that *I'm better, more important, more intelligent. My time matters more than yours. My work is more valuable. Where I'm going is more important than where everyone else on the road is going. I don't care what everyone else needs right now, I have to have this. What I'm doing matters more. I'm at the center of the world.* Few of us would come out and say those things, and many of us wouldn't even be aware that these thoughts are driving us. But at some level and to some degree, every human being has had them.

It took quite a while for me to learn this hard lesson. I have a gift of leadership and an analytical mind, and I read and absorb a lot of information. Over the years, especially as a young pastor, I had to make a lot of decisions from my analysis of the information I'd gathered. I also had a lot of smart people around me to help. But I eventually came to the realization that when I analyzed and evaluated something and got good counsel, my perspective became *the* perspective—the right one. I was sincere, convinced I was objective, and began to confuse "my perspective" with the truth.

God kindly and powerfully revealed the depth of a pride I was completely unaware of. I found myself in a couple of situations where I had done my research, connected all the dots, put together a solid evaluation, and ended up being embarrassingly, devastatingly wrong because I was missing a few pieces of information or had overlooked something in my analysis. My self-reliance, self-confidence, and unconscious grandiosity took a huge hit.

I remember having a back-and-forth with the Lord, which I'll never forget, that I sensed went something like: "Chip, you have an analytical mind," He affirmed. "You evaluate everything. You have some good gifts. Your discernment can be very helpful. You connect all the dots and come to your conclusions. And when you're done, do you know what you have?"

I knew better than to answer that question. "No, Lord. What do I have?"

"You have *your perspective*. That's all!"

I had to come to grips with the fact that even though what I brought to the table was valuable, it wasn't the only valuable perspective. And it wasn't failsafe. Many of my assumptions were based on and biased by my pride.

Living as though we are the center of our own world is unloving and lethal to our relationships.

We can clothe our prideful thoughts with all kinds of Bible verses and Christian justifications with our gifts and insights, schedules, ministry goals, a need to feel significant, and image management—believe me, I know—yet still be nurturing pride beneath it all. When we crave everyone's approval or position ourselves to impress others—or feel ashamed or embarrassed that we haven't been successful at impressing the right people—that's empty conceit. Pride is rearing its ugly head.

This is so deeply rooted in our flesh that we can't just try to manage it. We have to attack it. We have to put it to death (Gal. 5:24). We need to become very aware of our own thought patterns, and whenever pride (or wounded pride) pops up, identify it for what it is, confess it, repent, and crucify it. Living as though we are the center of our own world is unloving and lethal to our relationships. It destroys them and us in the process.

Attacking pride puts us in sync with God's will. Scripture tells and shows us frequently that He opposes the proud but gives grace to the humble (Prov. 3:34; 1 Peter 5:5; James 4:6). These are two of Scripture's most reliable guardrails—God brings the proud down and builds the humble up. In fact, God says that even though He dwells in a high and holy place, He also dwells with the contrite and lowly of spirit (Isa. 57:15). Proud hearts are always eventually thwarted, but whenever anyone comes to God with a broken spirit and contrite heart, no matter what terrible thing they've done, they are flooded with grace, forgiveness, and restoration.

I've had to learn to purge my thoughts and opinions of my pride when faced with a difficult conversation. All of us have to have hard conversations sometimes, whether it's with family members, employers or employees, or fellow church members. It's easy to come across as though our perspective is completely right and we assume that the other person is wrong.

Over the years, I developed a script for myself to help me "speak the truth in love" and not assume that "my perception" = "the truth." It goes something like this: "Hey friend, I think we need to talk about something, okay? I have some concerns and just want to share my perspective with you. I don't want you to assume what I'm about to say is the truth because I don't know if it is. But I have a deep concern and care about you very much." Then I outline the behaviors or the attitudes that need to be addressed from my perspective and say, "Now, I could be wrong. Believe me, I've been wrong before. But would you take this to the Lord and ask Him if what I've shared with you has any validity? And if so, act accordingly and let's get back together and talk about it." That approach—acknowledging that I might perceive things inaccurately—has changed the course of my life and my relationships.

Our ministry has partnered with a wide variety of people around the world from different cultural and theological backgrounds, and I've come to realize over time that we can learn so much from people we might disagree with on secondary matters. I strongly believe we need to agree on core doctrines of our faith (the Apostles' Creed), but I greatly appreciate the variety of perspectives that come out of those foundational truths. I love the reverence and high view of God I see in my Reformed brothers and sisters, and I love the expectation of my charismatic brothers and sisters that God is actually going to intervene supernaturally. I love the evangelistic zeal of missions-focused denominations and the compassion of those focused on the practical needs of the poor and oppressed. I've been in churches that worship through a quiet, reverent awe and those that worship through exuberant celebration.

I want to get close to all of these people to learn from them. I don't have to agree with everything they believe or do, but if the Holy Spirit is willing to work through them—and He is—then I want to learn to grow from their unique perspective and experience.

Judgmental attitudes are one sign of pride.

As a younger pastor, I made a lot of critical judgments about people or groups who thought about and did things differently. With every positive attribute, I saw a negative that I needed to be very careful to avoid. I prided myself on my orthodoxy and commitment to God's Word, yet like the Pharisees of old, I was critical and unloving within. Do you know what that kind of hyper-discernment represents? Pride. The diverse body of Christ is beautiful. He's the head, but the body has many parts with different roles and purposes. We are called to build up the entire body—within our own congregations and between them.

Judgmental attitudes are one sign of pride, but there are others. When we find ourselves getting defensive in the middle of a conversation . . . when we make excuses for a mistake so it doesn't reflect too badly on us . . . when we blame someone else for a problem we had a hand in creating . . . when we demand our rights . . . when we interrupt other people because we have to get our opinion out right away . . . when we carelessly arrive late because our time is

> **Pride is rooted in our deep insecurities.**

so important . . . when we talk more than we listen . . . all of these are signs of pride rising out of our subconscious and coming to the surface.

I remember being in a marriage counseling session with Theresa many years ago, and the counselor was trying to help us communicate better. We were talking about what wasn't working well, and Theresa looked straight at me and said something that stung me and stuck with me because I could hear the pain in her voice: "Chip just always has to have the last word." And she was right.

Pride is rooted in our deep insecurities. We feel a need to prove ourselves, show our stuff, manage our reputation, and present the right image. We think we need to do that to be accepted, but it actually pushes people away. This may come as a surprise, but God is not the only one opposed to the proud. So is everyone else. We don't like seeing pride in anyone, including ourselves. We are drawn to gentle spirits, honesty and authenticity, an openness to listen, and a willingness to be vulnerable. The humble own their junk, and people connect and want to be around those who are genuinely humble.

CHOOSE TO PRACTICE HUMILITY

At this point, I'm sure God has given you a number of nudges about some of the pride in your life. You're not alone, and the Holy Spirit convicts us not to make us feel bad, but to bring life, hope, and change. The question is, how do we respond? Simply trying hard to be humbler never works—we need to "go into training" to cultivate a humble heart. And training requires practice. We must build habits and rhythms into our daily lives that create a "putting others first" mindset. I've seen that kind of humility even in the business world, in places where I would not have expected to find it. A friend, a venture capitalist in Silicon Valley who invested early in companies that are now worth billions, is a humble follower of Jesus. Every day, he goes to his office and writes three thank-you notes before he does anything else at his desk, just so he can affirm the people he works with. It's a simple, deliberate practice that puts his focus on others and gratitude in his heart for who they are.

I've had meetings with others in that world and learned quickly that "late" is anathema to them, so when I had a meeting with this same friend at a coffee shop, I showed up ten minutes early. I got my coffee, only to discover that he was already sitting at a table in the corner. Why does a billionaire whose time is precious arrive fifteen minutes early to a meeting with a friend? "Chip, I didn't want to waste any of your time"—as if my time was more valuable than his. He was ready. I had written out questions, and he had already prepared answers. He was modeling a clear message: that I mattered to him.

Do you see the connection? Two seemingly little practices (writing notes and being early to meetings) have created a mindset in a man who could very easily think that his money, position, and reputation make him more important than others. That's a beautiful example of humility. It isn't just an emotion or a self-assessment of whether you're a big shot or not. It's noticing the needs of other people and meeting them, honoring them with your attention, hearing their concerns, and supporting and encouraging them. It takes some consistent self-training to do that, but those who are faithful even in little things will become faithful in bigger things (Luke 16:10). We have multiple opportunities to practice humility every day. Start with something small and focus on being consistent. Practicing humility requires intentionality and discipline, but it pays great rewards.

Paul framed it in terms of putting the needs and interests of other people ahead of our own—not because our needs and interests aren't important, but because God has designed community to work in such a way that everyone best gets their needs met when we look out for each other's interests rather than when we focus on our own. If everyone is focused on their own needs, we're the only ones supporting ourselves. If everyone is focused on each other's needs, ours are met from multiple directions. He created us for that kind of mutual support.

When I went into "humility training" years ago, it was because I finally realized what my exaggerated sense of importance had done to me. I would weave through traffic to arrive twenty seconds ahead of the people I passed several miles back. I'd get to the grocery lines and figure out instantly which cashiers were slow, how many people were in line, how full their baskets were, and which line would get me through checkout the quickest. And even though I'd sometimes save a few minutes here and there, I realized that trying to prioritize my interest, and get my way and optimize my experience, produced constant stress.

I learned from some great thinkers and writers about the importance of slowing life down and focusing on others. So I went into humility training. Now, I *choose* to make a few small but radical changes that force me to put others first. It was terribly hard at first, but it ended up being a life-changing, two-year journey. First, I decided to drive in the right lane and let other people pass me; second, to get in the longest grocery store or bank line; and third, to make a point of finding out who cleaned restrooms and thank them for their work. They were very little things to people on the road or in a line, but big things in the eyes of God and the people who feel affirmed and blessed by them. Over time, slowing down became a habit.

SOME SPECIFIC WAYS TO PRACTICE HUMILITY

There are several practical steps we can take to learn humility:

First, *observe*. Notice what's going on. Look at the people around you and recognize who would benefit by getting in line in front of you or being seated at the next open table. Slow down to let someone in front of you when they're trying to get on a busy expressway or change lanes. Graciously defer to others when you see their need. This doesn't come naturally to most of us.

Most people are not truly present where they are, so they don't give themselves the opportunity to notice the needs around them. They are physically present, of course, but they aren't spiritually, emotionally, and relationally present. I get sad when I see several people at a table, and all of them are on their phones and not interacting with each other—even though I have been one of those people. We need to check emails and texts sometimes, but often looking at our phones is just a habit or an impulse to fill up empty time. We risk missing the opportunities God has placed right in front of us because we're distracted with other things. I challenge you to take one small step to disengage from your phone. Perhaps leave it in the car when running errands. Better yet, put it in a basket on silent mode before dinner so you're not interrupted; even better, set it in another room after 7 p.m. to have a quiet night.

I challenge you to take one small step to disengage from your phone.

Sometimes we assume becoming genuinely humble demands some huge moment of sacrifice and selflessness; and on occasion it might, but it's in the everyday little things that character is developed and people are blessed.

I was at a conference recently and was trying to plug in a device. There were wires everywhere because many people were charging their devices, and there were no available outlets. An acquaintance came up—I knew him but not very well—and we exchanged hellos. It was a brief interaction, and I didn't give it any further thought.

The next week, I received a delivery—a little recharging station that I could plug my device into next time I needed to. There was no note, and I even had to think back to figure out where it came from. That's what other-centered humility looks like. This guy saw a need and met it. That's a great way to delight someone's heart, and it's contagious. It fosters a climate of love.

Second, *listen*. This isn't easy for those of us who are very verbal. We like to talk. But try just listening sometimes, and listen to understand, not to respond with your opinion. Ask follow-up questions, like why they felt the way they did in that situation, what concerns they have about whatever they're going through, or simply ask if you can be of any help.

Can you imagine what would happen if you set aside an hour every two to three days just to focus on other people? Maybe you go stand in line where people are and see what conversations come up, or you look around and find someone to talk to. If you ask a couple of questions, you might find out what's really going on in their life. I've struck up a casual conversation like that while waiting in line and found out the person had cancer or was struggling with a huge burden, and I was able to offer encouragement and prayer. Sometimes I find a quiet corner and ask God to bring people to my mind who need encouragement. I sit quietly and listen, and whoever the Holy Spirit brings to my mind, I call or text something simple, thoughtful, and encouraging such as, "Hey friend, just sitting here in the coffee shop and the Lord brought you to mind. Prayers for you today."

Third, *serve.* Start with the little things. Who gets to watch which channel? Where are we going out to eat? Who cleans up to get ready for the big meeting? Who needs to know someone is praying for them? These little things build up the muscle of humility and lead to greater opportunities to serve, honor, and edify the people around you.

God's grace flows toward humility. It's not about belittling yourself, considering yourself unimportant, or letting people take advantage of you. It doesn't mean you never get to have a say or always have to adapt yourself to the dominating personalities around you. And please don't confuse humility with passivity or being unwilling to share your own thoughts and opinions. Rather, it's a posture of honoring, affirming, and serving other people as an expression of Jesus' love for them. Spiritually humble people carry an attitude within themselves that constantly says, "I am second. You can be first; I'll release my rights and be second. I'd rather honor our friendship than prove I'm important, better, or right."

Practice saying that: *"I am second."* Embrace it as a mindset. Approach all of your relationships with that perspective. Don't belittle yourself—you have a lot to offer, including the Spirit of Christ working within you—but don't promote yourself above the other person in your own mind. Be content with your second-ness.

Can you envision what a world full of magnanimous, deferential, servant-hearted people would look like? Can you imagine how people who don't know Jesus would respond to believers who make it a priority to be kind, winsome, gracious, gentle, and courteous? That's how we spread the aroma of Christ in this world, and it's powerful. And make no mistake, this is how you can change your world, your home, your school, your family, your marriage, your workplace, your church, and your ministry.

LOVE THAT CHANGES THE WORLD

That's the ultimate expression of "love gives." This is step number one for every Christian and for every church in changing the world. Preaching the gospel message without a heart overflowing with love doesn't accomplish much. Telling people Jesus loves them without embodying and demonstrating His love isn't very persuasive. Declaring the truth without wrapping it in authentic, heartfelt, Spirit-empowered love is fruitless. Our highest calling, above all others we might imagine, is to love God with everything in us and love others as ourselves. If we don't do that, we miss our purpose.

Declaring the truth without wrapping it in authentic, heartfelt, Spirit-empowered love is fruitless.

The world is in desperate need of this kind of love. It has no shortage of people competing for their own agendas and interests. It doesn't need anyone else to enter the fray with a heart toward self-promotion. What it needs is people who seek to be powerfully, persistently, adamantly humble and loving in their desire to bring unity to the church and compassion to the broken and hurting.

God is pleased with humble hearts that are filled with love. He knows we can't become that kind of person without His help, but He is more than willing to help. When we *choose* to rely on Him and ask to be filled with His generous, giving love, His heart is filled with joy. Not surprisingly, so are ours.

QUESTIONS FOR REFLECTION/DISCUSSION

1. What does "declaring war" on selfishness look like in your life? Discuss the "paradox" of servant living and personal joy.

2. What specific step is God leading you to take to declare war on selfishness in your life?

3. What story about going into "humility training" resonated most with you? Why?

4. Why does humility require practice? What simple habit might you begin to create an "I am second" mindset?

Part 2: Love Serves

When he had finished washing their feet, he put on his clothes and returned to his place. "Do you understand what I have done for you?" he asked them. "You call me 'Teacher' and 'Lord,' and rightly so, for that is what I am. Now that I, your Lord and Teacher, have washed your feet, you also should wash one another's feet. I have set you an example that you should do as I have done for you.

John 13: 12-15

CHAPTER 3

Love Serves

Unless you zipped past the questions at the end of the last chapter, I'm guessing you got hit right between the eyes in the same way that I do every time I take a hard look at the level of selfishness and pride in my life. Yes, it is a lifelong journey; but we can make real progress. We can learn to walk humbly with God and experience the joy of giving as His Spirit working in us creates a desire to put others first and to become increasingly kind, generous, caring people.

We love people who have those qualities, and I believe as disciples of Jesus we all long for more of that gentle, humble, loving focus that I discussed in the last chapter. But there's a problem, and it's a big one. What are we to do with those competing desires that we all have to be *great*?

I'm not talking about that arrogant, "I want to be the center of the world's attention" kind of great, and putting everyone down along the way; I'm talking about those legitimate God-given intrinsic desires to:

– Be successful in what we do.

– Be esteemed by those who matter.

– Be valued for who we are.

– Be significant and fulfill a godly purpose.

– Be admired for the right reasons.

– Be known and appreciated.

– Accomplish a worthy task.

– Fulfill a God-given calling.

– Excel in developing our talents and gifts . . . to honor God, meet people's needs, and experience a healthy sense of meaningful accomplishment for the right reasons.

If we failed to take these things into consideration, we can find ourselves in a no-win situation with some false beliefs that bring about a lot of pain. I've seen people take some very anti-productive and damaging paths toward seeking to be humble and getting rid of their pride. The fact of the matter is, when we become hyper-focused on getting rid of our pride, we are focusing on ourselves yet again. So how do we balance this God-given desire for greatness and the scriptural command to walk humbly with our God (Mic. 6:8)? Answering that question is what this chapter is all about.

For context, I am one of those people who went about seeking to be humble in a dysfunctional way that almost destroyed my relationship with the Lord. I was so aware of my prideful thoughts, actions, and motives that I beat myself up all the time. I tried very hard in the early days of my Christian life to think humble thoughts, to say humble things, and to put others first, only to be constantly frustrated and overwhelmed by the realization that my focus was always coming back to being on *me*. I became ultra-introspective, was discouraged, and began to think the Christian life must not be for me or I'm wasn't worthy to even try to live it. I didn't know much theology, and I had not yet even read through the New Testament, but what I did know was my plan and desire to walk humbly with God was a train wreck.

For those of you who may have deep struggles with pride, a little background on my story might be a help to you. My parents wanted to have five boys; they only got one and that was after having two girls. My father was an exceptional athlete, marine, WWII veteran, and functioning alcoholic whose focus was to make me *great*.

I remember learning to start reading at three years old, diving off a ten-foot board at four, making the little league majors' baseball team for ten- to twelve-year-olds at eight. My dad pushed me hard, told me I could be president one day, and had harsh criticism for me when I didn't measure up.

Unfortunately, I was skinny and undersized at five feet tall in the seventh grade. I went out for the basketball team and was told I would do better at wrestling—as the team needed someone in the eighty-five-pound weight class.

Fast-forward, I took that challenge and my family-of-origin dysfunction and developed a hyper-focused, driven, take-no-prisoners attitude to become an excellent basketball player and earn a college scholarship for basketball. I had heard of a 5'9" basketball guard just a few years older who led the nation in scoring; I reasoned if he could make it in basketball, so could I.

I practiced basketball seven or eight hours a day. I thought about it even when I wasn't playing. I played pickup ball with guys four or five years older than me. I talked them into driving into the inner city so we could play against better, more competitive pickup ball players. I was incredibly focused round the clock because my goal was to get a basketball scholarship.

After all that work, along with a growth spurt, I became a very good basketball player by the time I was a senior in high school.

I stepped up my dedication. I even broke up with a girl right before that season so I could focus on my singular goal. I told her there was no room for anything in my life other than basketball. It was unkind, insensitive, and highly self-focused. In my effort to prove my value and worth to my father, I developed a mindset that I can do "whatever it takes" when I have a desire to be great at something. I knew I had what it took to devote everything to that all-consuming goal and make everything and everyone else secondary. Read that sentence again, slowly. It's filled with "I can" be great if "I work hard enough." I did and it worked, but it warped my soul.

But deep down inside, God has planted within us an innate desire to be significant and accomplish great things.

In this chapter, we'll talk about a positive approach to walking humbly with God that doesn't focus on ourselves, but actually ties into that God-given desire to be great. We will learn from Jesus' example and His teaching a very different paradigm for greatness to be achieved and humility to be embraced.

I believe we all want to be great. Not everyone believes they can be great at something—many have given up on that dream, some so long ago that they can hardly remember—but deep down inside, God has planted within us an innate desire to be significant and accomplish great things.

You may remember when you were a child being asked what you wanted to be when you grew up. Whatever the answer was—an astronaut, a firefighter, a police officer, a pilot, a star athlete, a famous actor or singer, or even a mom or dad—you probably envisioned being great at it. As you grew, the specifics of that ambition may have changed, but the hope of being significant and successful likely didn't.

Over time, that desire can be quenched by hard circumstances and harsh words or dismissed as unrealistic. Life chips away at our ideals. But somewhere deep inside, the God who made us in His image and put eternity in our hearts still nurtures our longing to be great.

Our desire for greatness shows up in many ways both big and small. We want to look our best, do our best, and be seen in the best light. This is certainly born out of pride at times; but a sanctified holy ambition for our lives to count, to make a difference, is God-given and we all have a desire for transcendence.

Does that sound prideful? We spent the last chapter talking about humility as the foundation to love; and now we're talking about a God-given desire to be great. Isn't that a huge contradiction?

Not at all. I believe the quest for greatness is universal because God made us in His image, and everything He does is great. The skies, stars, seas, mountains, all of creation is great. And human beings are at the pinnacle of that creation to serve as reflections of His image. We were designed for greatness. The challenge is how to get there.

And that's where pride and humility come in. The path God has given us to become great isn't what our instincts tell us it should be. Human pride entered the world when we sinned, and from that point forward we've taken it upon ourselves to define greatness by the world's standards and achieve it on our own terms. Scripture is filled with examples, from the Tower of Babel (Gen. 11:1–9) onward, of self-sufficient people trying to make a name for themselves. History and our own eyes tell us of leaders, warriors, creators, scholars, and countless other ambitious people

We were designed for greatness. The challenge is how to get there.

who are driven to be more, do more, and have more. We want to measure greatness, figure out who is great and who isn't, and compare ourselves to see where we are on the scale. The quest for greatness is universal.

The problem is that we've distorted that God-given desire and measured it in all the wrong ways.

HOW DO WE MEASURE GREATNESS?

James and John, two of Jesus' closest disciples, wanted to be great. Their mother wanted them to be great too. So, they came to Jesus with a request: to sit at His right and left hand in the kingdom. Then the other disciples became indignant and got into an argument over which of them was the greatest (Mark 10:35–40; Luke 22:24).

We might have rebuked these disciples for their arrogance in wanting to be great, but Jesus never did. He never told them that they needed to be more modest, that humility required them to belittle themselves or fade into the background, or anything else that would tame their desire for significance. He simply reframed their thinking about greatness. "Are you able to drink the cup that I drink, or to be baptized with the baptism with which I am baptized?" He asked them (Mark 10:38). Then He gave them a new paradigm:

> "You know that those who are recognized as rulers of the Gentiles lord it over them; and their great men exercise authority over them. But it is not this way among you, but whoever wishes to become great among you shall be your servant; and whoever wishes to be first among you shall be slave of all. For even the Son of Man did not come to be served, but to serve, and to give His life a ransom for many." (Mark 10:42–45)

Did you catch that? "Whoever wishes to become great . . ." He's giving us the key. Not only can we be great; we are called to greatness. But how God measures greatness and the way to get there isn't what most of us would have expected.

What Jesus is saying, in other words, is that if you want to go up, you need to go down. If you want to be first, you need to be last. It isn't wrong to be great. God gives us dreams, desires, ambitions, and passions. He just points us in a counterintuitive direction to get us there.

In our fallen humanness, we measure greatness in all sorts of ways:

- ***Power***—We measure greatness by who and what we control. By human standards, great people have great power and authority. We measure power in huge companies and organizations, but also even in local communities and small groups.

- ***Possessions***—We measure greatness by how much we have and how prestigious the sizes, models, brands, and quality are. We think more possessions and more buying power gets us a life with greater freedom. The greatest people live in the biggest houses on the highest hills with the best view and fill their lives with the highest quality of things.

- ***Position***—We measure greatness by our roles and responsibilities and work our way up the ladder to higher and higher positions. This is closely related to power and prestige, but we frame it in terms of upward mobility. We expend a lot of effort trying to climb ladders into greater and greater positions because we can hardly imagine going any direction other than up.

- ***Prestige***—We measure greatness by how many people look up to us, how high we are in the pecking order, and how much influence we have—relationally, socially, financially, and even spiritually. The more likes and followers we have, the more influence we have. We wear and drive and display things—logos, degrees, trophies, styles—that let people know who we are and what we've done.

• ***Productivity***—We measure greatness by how much we accomplish. Our achievements—buildings built, games won, deals made, quotas reached and exceeded, children reared, people influenced—offer visible proof that we have done great things. When we look back over our lives, we want to see tangible evidence that we made a difference.

We're used to these measures of greatness. This is just how life works, isn't it? Except sometimes it doesn't.

HOW DO WE OBTAIN GREATNESS?

A girl born in 1910 grew up to become a teacher. For most of her life, she owned almost nothing and sought no recognition, but by the time she died, she had three thousand followers who had started institutions just like hers and influenced millions of people. Her name was Agnes Gonxha Bojaxhiu, and we know her now as Mother Teresa. She won the Nobel Peace Prize, and by virtually all accounts is considered a great woman. But she didn't become great by following the path most people pursue.

Mother Teresa didn't seem to care what people thought of her. She once spoke at a prayer breakfast in Washington, DC, and called out the president of the United States and other leaders on the issue of the sanctity of life. She didn't depend on people's opinions for her self-esteem or sense of accomplishment. She wasn't trying to climb the world's ladders of success. She had a lot of influence and used it wisely, but she never sought influence simply for the sake of having it. As Jesus taught, she became great through humility and service.

There's no reason to feel guilty about your desire for greatness. But as we can see from the lives of people pursuing power, possessions, position, prestige, and productivity, as well as from the lives of people like Mother Teresa, there are two ways to seek it—two roads we can travel on our quest to become great.

TWO ROADS TO GREATNESS

One way to become great is to try to *ascend into it.* This is how you become great by the world's measuring stick and within its systems. You ascend by getting more money, more education, more power and prestige, a more youthful appearance, a lot of busyness, all the accolades that come with it, and all the other trappings of success. The metrics are everywhere, and we are tempted to believe they reflect true greatness. *Forbes* and *Fortune* magazines tell us the fifty richest people in the world; TMZ and *Entertainment Tonight* give us the inside scoop on celebrities and how beautiful people live; *People* magazine lets us know who the "sexiest" man and woman alive are; and the list goes on and on. Most of us don't end up with overwhelming riches, power, and fame, but all of us have been brainwashed to some degree to see these as the measure of greatness.

There's nothing wrong with those external things. Ideally, this is not an either/or proposition. I know plenty of very humble people who have them and steward them well, but they don't define greatness. In fact, we should hope and pray God entrusts many of His people with extraordinary resources and positions of authority to do great things for His glory. I'm thrilled that God has put many of His servants in very powerful positions in business and government. We need kingdom-minded people in all kinds of spheres of influence to advance the kingdom and help it flourish. But they would agree that greatness comes not in having a lot but in serving God with what we have.

Greatness comes not in having a lot but in serving God with what we have.

The other way to obtain greatness is to *descend into it*. That's what Jesus taught us—not to become great by ascending but by descending. And the way to descend into it is through servanthood that is motivated by love. That's how Mother Teresa obtained her greatness and how numerous believers throughout history have become great in God's kingdom. Many have looked insignificant and irrelevant to people who have bought into the world's system of greatness, but in God's eyes, they are highly esteemed.

According to his biographer Arnold A. Dallimore, George Whitefield, the great revival preacher and evangelist of the eighteenth century, once prayed, "God make me an extraordinary Christian." He didn't want to be an average Christian or even just a good Christian. He wanted to be a great Christian, and God answered his prayer.[2]

Have you ever thought of praying that prayer? Among whatever other ambitions you might have, is that one of them? After all, there must be great Christians somewhere, people God is using mightily for His purposes—not because they are great in themselves but they are great because God has made them so. Would you consider praying that same prayer to see what God does with it? Have you ever considered that God is actually longing for His people to want to be great—like James and John did—and then to follow their example?

I believe God will answer that prayer if you are sincere in it, and it will have nothing to do with your apparent qualifications or your track record. You can rest assured that this is not a matter of resources, education, or background, and it certainly isn't a matter of your history. Just look at all the people God used in Scripture:

• **Jacob**, a manipulator who deceived his father and his brother to get his brother's all-important blessing, connived to get his brother's birthright, and fled to another country to avoid his brother's wrath.

• **Moses**, who murdered a man and lived in self-imposed exile for forty years because he was no longer welcome in Egypt.

• **Rahab**, who had a history as a prostitute but recognized Israel's God as the true one.

• **David**, who committed adultery with Bathsheba and had her husband, one of his most loyal friends, killed to cover it up.

• **Solomon**, who was given amazing wisdom (along with power and wealth) by God and built Israel's first temple, yet made unholy alliances and compromised his faith at pagan shrines.

• **Paul**, who persecuted Christians and zealously tried to stamp out the Christian movement before he met Jesus.

• **Matthew**, who had exploited his fellow Jews as a tax collector for the Romans and was considered a traitor among his own people.

• **Peter**, who was impetuous and unstable, often opening his mouth when he shouldn't, often misunderstanding situations and the teachings of Jesus, and even denying Jesus when the pressure was on.

• **James and John**, who seem to have had anger-management issues and wanted to call down fire from heaven to judge their opponents.

This list could go on and on. If you've ever thought you might be disqualified, it should be clear from those biblical heroes that you aren't. God called them and transformed them in spite of their flaws. Believe me, you qualify. And don't think because I used biblical examples that you need to be a spiritual superstar. I know one person whose deepest desire was to be a great mom. Then I got to marry her. I have a daughter who is gifted in many ways, and because she wanted to be a great mom too, she set aside some significant opportunities to invest in her children. I've met ordinary people who wanted to be great performers or athletes to share the gospel, some who wanted to launch great businesses that change lives, and others who dreamed and started great ministries that change the world.

When we catch a vision of what greatness in God's kingdom looks like and how we can obtain it, our priorities change. Like this short, skinny junior high basketball player learned long ago, we know how to put everything aside when we really want to pursue a worthy goal. With that kind of focus, we can become great in God's kingdom. But only when we learn where true greatness is really found.

I never became a pro basketball player, but I did go to college on a basketball scholarship and later got to play against Olympic teams all over South America. I was able to share Christ with many people through those experiences, which God used to call me into what I'm doing today. Once I learned the direction of greatness, descending into it rather than exhausting myself by trying to ascend into it, God worked through my desire to lead me into fruitfulness.

HOW IS TRUE GREATNESS ACHIEVED?

Paul defines true greatness in Philippians 2:3–4, which we explored in the last chapter, and it should come as no surprise that his definition fits perfectly with what Jesus taught His disciples. When Paul instructed these believers to do nothing from selfishness or pride, but instead to view each other with humility and honor, prioritizing each other's interests over their own, he was following the teaching of Jesus that greatness comes through serving. Considering others as more important than yourself and seeking to meet their needs before meeting your own is the epitome of greatness in God's kingdom.

Considering others as more important than yourself and seeking to meet their needs before meeting your own is the epitome of greatness in God's kingdom.

This follows naturally from what Paul wrote in the first two verses of this chapter, doesn't it? Serving is a response of love, the outflow of the affection and compassion believers are to have for one another. Love not only gives. It serves.

So, the way God measures greatness is not by the values of this world but by the priorities of His kingdom.

And the way we obtain it is not by ascending a ladder of power and success but by descending into greatness by humility and servanthood.

And so humility is the key to greatness. Humility is the channel through which the supernatural power of God's love flows to heal our deepest hurts and restore our most important relationships.

Humility is the channel through which the supernatural power of God's love flows to heal our deepest hurts and restore our most important relationships.

That's a highly relevant message for a church that was being divided by competing interests and agendas—and therefore highly relevant to Christians today. The antidote to the factionalism that had been developing in that congregation was not for Paul to choose sides and declare who was right—that would have made matters worse—but to reintroduce the love, humility, and servanthood of Jesus into their fellowship. That's a powerful principle in any era.

What does that look like in action? Paul modeled that message himself, not only in this letter to the Philippians but in many of his other letters as well. He lived out the power of this truth.

But Paul knew of a much greater example too. In the next chapter, we will enter into one of the most sacred and unfathomable passages in Scripture. Paul not only instructs the Philippians in the ways of humility, service, and love; he also presents to them the ultimate model to follow.

Pray for a spirit of wisdom as we dive into the astonishing depths and heights of that example. You'll need divine insight because it stretches our understanding and defies our explanations. Our finite intellects can barely grasp the meaning of it, even on the surface. But when we embrace this example, even with our limited understanding, it has the power to revolutionize our lives and heal our relationships, both for our well-being and the glory of God.

QUESTIONS FOR REFLECTION/DISCUSSION

1. Is there anything wrong with wanting to be great? Successful?

2. How has your family background or life experiences helped or hurt your desire to be great in God's eyes and not the world's?

3. How do most people measure greatness? How does God measure it?

4. What are the two roads to greatness outlined in this chapter? On which road are you currently traveling?

CHAPTER 4

Following Jesus into Greatness

The story I'm about to tell is true, but it's a collage of a number of men that I've met with privately who shared honestly and deeply, and often with tears.

I was asked to speak at one of the most exclusive country clubs in the world. The host was a godly man who cared deeply about the spiritual destiny and spiritual growth of his friends. He launched a number of Bible studies at this club and others like it, inspiring business owners and former CEOs, who are now mostly retired, to use their gifts and strengths to build God's kingdom.

He had some encouraging success in helping these wealthy and powerful leaders to discover their purpose after their corporate achievements, but the great majority of those at this club were spending the last season of their life chasing pleasure and looking for meaning. Private conversations revealed heartache, unresolved issues with grown children, depression, and deep regrets. He asked me to come and share a bold message about God's purpose for those to whom He's entrusted much wealth, power, leadership, intelligence, and influence. With unusual boldness that I can only credit to the Holy Spirit, I talked about a very sad day that may be coming at the judgment seat of Christ for followers of Jesus who have been given much but did little with it. I was kind and sought to reveal God's heart and help them see that they were missing out on God's wonderful plans for their lives and millions were missing out on the impact they could be having if their time and wealth and leadership were channeled in this last season of their life.

As people were enjoying hors d'oeuvres and cocktails after my message, it was obvious that some were uncomfortable and others deeply moved. One of the wealthiest and most powerful attendees approached me with watery eyes and thanked me for what I shared, but thought it was too late for him. "I was a CEO of one of the largest companies in the world, made millions of dollars, traveled all over the world with my job, and now find myself with many regrets. I've given some money to Christian causes, and I know I've received Jesus personally, but I've not done anything with my life with the kind of kingdom focus that you described." He was vulnerable and honest, and I was shocked as I did not know him well at all. In a moment of tenderness, I looked him in the eye and said, "It may be late, but you need to remember that God is never finished with us until He takes us home. Moses didn't get started in his ministry until he was eighty; I'm sure He's more than willing to do the same for you."

What was ironic about that evening and many like it was that I've experienced that conversation multiple times with people whom "everyone would want to be like"—wealthy, powerful, multiple homes, private jets, go anywhere anytime and do or buy whatever you want, etc.

They ascended the ladder of success like very few, but the outcomes were far different than they expected. The success and wealth and power didn't satisfy. The casualties were often a marriage or two that didn't work out and lack of any real relationship with their adult children or grandchildren. It was sad; they had gained the whole world and forfeited their very lives. Their ladder was leaning against the wrong wall.

It might surprise you that God wants you and me to be great.

We've established that the desire for greatness is universal.

We've also established that it's not wrong to be great.

The real issue is how do you get there. Which wall is your ladder leaning on? The ladder of ascent that leads to worldly power, prestige, position, possessions, and hyper productivity; or the ladder of descent into greatness via humility, selflessness, love, and sacrifice as you give your life away?

It might surprise you that God wants you and me to be great. Great in His eyes! That may or may not come with any worldly success or the perks by which the world measures success. God has different plans for different people and knows what we can handle or what will corrupt us. In this chapter, we will learn *the path* of true greatness as we follow Jesus' example.

"Have this attitude in yourselves which was also in Christ Jesus." This profound, challenging command in Philippians 2:5 introduces one of Scripture's most beautiful and staggering passages. The words that follow in verses 6–11 are a poetic description of Jesus' descent from heaven to earth and back again in humility, service, and greatness. This may have been one of the church's earliest hymns, or Paul may have simply been inspired to express this astonishing image in the most elevated language he could think of. Either way, these words are an everlasting monument to the love and humility of Jesus that we are all called to embrace.

If you really want to know what humility looks like, Paul tells the Philippians, look at Jesus. He's the model. This is how you can achieve greatness, and how God changes you and uses you to change those around you so that your desire for greatness is satisfied and He gets the glory. Few know the blue-collar bricklayer who discipled me in college. He wasn't "great" in the world's eyes, but my life, family, and ministry as well as those of scores of others he and his wife discipled have had extraordinary impact on countless lives all around the world. Dave Marshall was one of the greatest men I've ever known.

Paul has urged the Philippians to be united in spirit because of the love they have for each other, then to look out for each other's interests and consider each other more important than themselves. Now he tells them to live from a particular mindset, as if to say, "Now that I have instructed you to be other-centered and not focus on yourself, here's how you should be thinking."

Our lives are shaped by what we think. "The mind set on the flesh is death, but the mind set on the Spirit is life and peace" (Rom. 8:6). So if we want change to happen, we won't get it by extraordinary self-effort or new information. We'll get it by changing the way we think (Rom. 12:2).

Humility flows from a specific mindset, and if God opposes the proud but gives grace to the humble, then our entire lives can rise and fall on our level of humility versus pride. Paul's words throughout Philippians point his readers in the direction of humility, and they are solid, profound instructions and explanations. But the Philippians need a picture. It's one thing to hear truth, another to see it in action. So Paul gives them the best picture they could ever imagine.

In presenting this picture, Paul walks us through all the ways the world measures success and then shows us how Jesus was great by a different measure—not by climbing the ladder, achieving great things, and gaining power and authority over people, but by *descending* into greatness. And because that's the path He took, God highly exalted Him above everyone and everything.

As we explore this passage in depth, I don't want you to get lost in the details. Before we dive in, take a moment to absorb the wide-angle view of the mystery of the incarnation:

> Have this attitude in yourselves which was also in Christ Jesus,
>
> who, although He existed in the form of God, did not regard equality with God a thing to be grasped,
>
> but emptied Himself, taking the form of a bond-servant, and being made in the likeness of men.
>
> Being found in appearance as a man, He humbled Himself by becoming obedient to the point of death, even death on a cross.
>
> For this reason also, God highly exalted Him, and bestowed on Him the name which is above every name,
>
> so that at the name of Jesus every knee will bow, of those who are in heaven and on earth and under the earth, and that every tongue will confess that Jesus Christ is Lord, to the glory of God the Father. (Phil. 2:5–11)

As we study this passage, I want you to see how antithetical Jesus' path is to the symbols and indicators we currently associate with greatness. In the pages that follow, I want to show you how counterintuitive and radically different Jesus' attitude is toward power, possessions, position, prestige, and productivity.

CHRIST'S ATTITUDE TOWARD POWER AND POSSESSIONS

We obtain true greatness when we embrace Jesus' attitude toward power and possessions, which is evident in the first line of this passage: "Although He existed in the form of God, [He] did not regard equality with God a thing to be grasped."

Literally, this tells us that Jesus existed in the form of God, but didn't see His deity as something to cling to. This word *form* is very important. We might think of it as an outward shape, but it really refers to the essential nature of something, its substance, what it actually is. Because Jesus existed in the form of God, He is therefore deity, fully God, the Creator of the universe.

In the incarnation—God coming to earth in the flesh—Jesus never rejected that role. He did not suddenly become un-God or anything less than divine. But in taking on a mindset of humility, He refused to keep His grip on all the privileges of deity.

Can you imagine? Jesus reigned in glory among myriad angels in the unimaginable beauty of heaven. He was worshiped and exalted as one with infinite power and wisdom. In another letter, Paul described Him as the image of the invisible God, the agent of creation of all things in heaven and on earth, visible and invisible, by whom everything was made and that He holds together by His powerful word (Col. 1:15–17). There is no higher authority in the universe.

Yet He left that glorious environment, took on human flesh, and lived among us as a suffering Servant because of His great love for us. Can you get your mind around that? Neither can I.

Think of all that Jesus had in His pre-incarnate being. He had all power and all possessions. He owned everything. "The earth is the LORD's, and all it contains, the world, and those who dwell in it" (Ps. 24:1). As Lord, Jesus ruled and reigned over it all. Yet He was willing to leave all of that on a mission to redeem and restore His wounded, broken, hurting creation. His love for humanity and His plan to save us prompted Him to let go of His power and possessions for a time and live as a limited human being on earth.

CHRIST'S ATTITUDE TOWARD POSITION AND PRESTIGE

Not only do we achieve true greatness when we embrace Jesus' attitude and mindset toward power and possessions; we also become truly great when we embrace His mindset toward position and prestige. He "emptied Himself, taking the form of a bond-servant, and being made in the likeness of men."

Do you see the exchange? He gave up the full privileges of deity in order to take on the form—again, not just the outward shape, but the essential nature—of a human being. And not just any human being but a bondservant, the lowest kind of servant assigned to perform the most menial and filthy tasks in a slave-holding household. Bondservants washed people's feet when they came in the door, cleaned the latrines, and did what other servants told them to do. Jesus didn't just descend a little bit. He descended into the depths. Jesus models that the way "up" is to first go "down."

The word for "emptied" has huge theological implications. In Greek, it's *kenosis* (literally "emptied out" or "depleted"), which means He made Himself as nothing. He didn't cease to be God in the flesh; His identity didn't change. But He veiled His glory. He voluntarily limited the use of His divine attributes.

In other words, Jesus gave up position and prestige in order to be made in the likeness of men. The Greek word for "likeness" is where we get the English words "scheme" and "schematic." This is an external form. Jesus was fully human, but He wasn't exactly like other humans. He had a pure human nature and was tempted in every way like we are, so He got the full human experience. But while fully human, He was also fully divine. This is what theologians call the hypostatic union. Jesus' incarnation was the union of undiminished deity and perfect humanity without confusion.

Jesus' incarnation was the union of undiminished deity and perfect humanity without confusion.

Because of His divinity, we tend to think that Jesus had an unfair advantage—that as a human being, He's an exception we can never live up to, not an example we can follow. Many of us therefore give up even trying to follow His example, assuming that if Jesus was Jesus and we are not, we can never follow Him completely. But the *kenosis,* His veiling of His deity, means He lived as a human being. When He lived out His life, it was pleasing the Father, but He didn't do it in His own strength. He fulfilled the law and the prophets and modeled for us how to be human, but He said He could do nothing on His own (John 5:30). He did all of His miraculous works and resisted all of His temptations "not only by being God, but also by being a human dependent on God." with "as the son of God fully dependent on the Father. The power at work within Him was from the power of the Spirit working through Him. That's why He's our example rather than our exception—which is exactly how Paul presents Him in this passage.

CHRIST'S ATTITUDE TOWARD PRODUCTIVITY

We become truly great not only by embracing Jesus' attitude and mindset toward power, possessions, position, and prestige, but also by embracing His mindset toward productivity. What did Jesus accomplish? "Being found in appearance as a man, He humbled Himself by becoming obedient to the point of death, even death on a cross."

That doesn't exactly fit our idea of the ladder to success, does it? In His humility, He became "obedient." Humility is not a feeling. It involves a different mindset, but it doesn't end in the mind. At its core, it's about obeying, expressing humility outwardly. And in Jesus' case, He expressed His obedient humility all the way to the point of death on a humiliating cross.

In our battle with pride, we must learn from Jesus' example. We will never defeat pride by focusing on pride. We've talked about attacking pride ruthlessly, but the most effective way to do that, once you recognize it working within you, is to turn your attention to the kind of attitude Jesus exemplified in becoming a servant. We overcome pride by replacing it with humility that seeks to serve, not to be served; seeks to give, not to get; and seeks to honor, rather than be honored.

This is one of the most powerful keys to transformation. The best way to change a thought pattern or behavior is not to focus on it but to replace it. Paul expressed this principle in Galatians 5:16: "Walk by the Spirit, and you will not carry out the desire of the flesh." Pride and humility work the same way. Walk in humility, and you won't gratify your own pride. When you walk into a room, be a servant. When you shop at a store, don't race to the front of the line. When your friends and family members need help, serve them. Substituting pride and the "me first" mindset of pride with the "I am second" mindset of humility is powerful.

As I wrote in the last chapter, this is a journey, and we have to train new thought patterns and behaviors. But be careful in your training not to become so focused on your battle that you reinforce pride rather than defeating it. I've tried so hard to be humble at times that I've realized the focus was still on me. I would throw pride out the door of my soul and it would come back through a window or the attic. I vividly remember describing my struggle with a seasoned leader who gave wise counsel, "Chip, stop focusing and worrying about being proud; just think and act like a servant with everyone in every situation. Jesus didn't *try* to be humble; He simply had a mindset focused on others, their needs and their struggles, and He served them. At times with food, other times with healing or forgiveness or comfort." So, just remember to focus on Him, not yourself, and put His humility into practice.

IN YOUR HUMILITY, PURSUE GREATNESS

When I was twenty-eight, I came to realize that much of my insecurities and workaholism rooted in my early years were all about productivity. I gained my sense of worth by accomplishing *much* in order to be valued and accepted, to be "great." After a brown-bag lunch with Professor Howard Hendricks and a small group of seminary students, I had an epiphany: "The greatest accomplishment" I could ever make in my life would not be how much I achieved, but what kind of person I became.

> "The greatest accomplishment" I could ever make in my life would not be how much I achieved, but what kind of person I became.

On the drive home from that lunch, I stopped at the Dairy Queen in Crandall. I was the only one there that afternoon. I found a corner, pulled out some napkins, and started making a "to be" list. I had created lots of "to do" lists, in which I prided myself on crossing off as many items as possible, as fast as possible each day. It produced a hurried, stressed out, over-achieving, self-focused servant of God. So that day I wrote in the quiet of a very common place who I *really* wanted to become. At the top of the list I wrote, "I want to be a great man of God."

Maybe that sounds arrogant, but would God want me to be an average man of God? I don't think so. I also don't think He would want me to be average in my other relationships either, so I continued on these sacred napkins that changed the course of my life: I want to be a great husband, a great father, a great friend, and a great pastor. I realized these "to be" goals would be impossible in my own strength and that my focus and entire schedule and priorities needed to change.

So, I wrote all of those "to be" goals into my schedule each week for decades. Little by little I've been training myself to be whom God wants me to be. I have a long way to go, but those "to be" goals were a radical mindset and attitude shift that put my ladder of what real success is on the right wall.

I've had the privilege of being around some people who have accomplished a lot. I've seen some turn to Jesus when they were in the pit, but I've also seen some turn to Him when they were at their peak and discovered that worldly success doesn't deliver on all its promises. In 2015, I had the opportunity to fill in for the chaplain of the Seattle Seahawks when they were in San Francisco for a game. The night before the game, fifteen guys on the team gathered for the chapel/Bible study. After I shared some thoughts with them on Romans 12, we began talking about surrender and being separate from the world's values as NFL athletes. The team had won the Super Bowl the year before, and their whole professional life had been geared toward that goal. But what happens after reaching it? Many players said that despite the joy and great accomplishment, an empty feeling was followed by a question, *That's it? Is that all there is?* These guys loved Jesus above all else, and they were honest that much of their identity and drive to be a Super Bowl champion had dominated their life, time, and decisions. And make no mistake—it was great—yet it was also hollow when weighed against the bigger issues of life, family, relationships, and God.

I once heard a prominent coach talk about a conversation with a group of Christian leaders who were also athletes and coaches. "Can anyone remember off the top of your head who won the Super Bowl five years ago?" one asked. They all had to get out their phones to look it up. The point is simple—the greatest worldly accomplishments in life are very transient, temporary and fleeting. Whether it's a Super Bowl, big job, corner office, your kids getting in the right school, or retiring with lots of money in the bank, the ladder on the wrong wall just can't deliver lasting greatness.

My point is not to say we shouldn't pursue excellence in everything we do. We absolutely should. But we need to remember what defines true greatness. In God's eyes, it's not championships, important titles, and capitalist ventures. It's loving others well. My desire is for God to look at me and say, "Chip, you're making progress. You're learning to love people the way I do." And I know the path toward that goal is humility, which is really hard for my personality and my flesh. But it's the only way.

So be aware of what you allow into your mind and whether it reflects the attitude of Jesus, who refused to cling to the privileges of deity, emptied Himself and veiled His glory, took the form of a bondservant, and became obedient to the point of death. Go into training to become servant-hearted. In every situation, learn to ask God who He wants you to love or help.

As you seek to develop the servant attitude of Jesus, consider these three characteristics of the mindset of a servant:

1. *No job is too low.* Jesus didn't consider any person or any task to be beneath Him. If there's trash on the ground, you pick it up. If the dishes need to be washed, you wash them. No job is too low, because your goal is to serve.

2. *No recognition is required.* True servants don't need to post their service on social media or get a pat on the back for what they do. They aren't looking for affirmation. They are focused on helping and affirming others.

3. *No thanks are required.* No one thanks a servant for doing what he's supposed to do. It's nice to be appreciated, but when we're serving in the name of Jesus and following His example, we know God sees. That's all we really need.

Can you imagine what this would look like at home, in the workplace, and at church? All of those environments would change dramatically, wouldn't they? The good news is that we can be a catalyst for change right now by embracing the servant mindset modeled by the humility of Jesus where we are.

THREE PRACTICES GREAT SERVANTS HAVE IN COMMON

1. *They observe needs.* True servants realize they aren't here to be served but to serve others, so they notice the needs of others. You'll see this at a really nice restaurant with servers who know how to serve. You don't have to tell them when to fill up your water because they have been watching attentively and see the need. You won't have to tell them when you're ready for the next course; they will notice and be prepared to put it on the table. They are aware of what's going on. That's how a servant observes.

2. *They take initiative.* They don't wait for a plea for help. A true servant is sensitive to the needs of others, takes the initiative without

being asked, and does what is necessary.

3. *They don't draw attention to themselves.* Jesus got a lot of attention, but not because He was flashy or sought it out. Sometimes He even told His followers not to be too vocal about what they had seen. He trusted the Father to accomplish His purposes at the right time.

In fact, we see this mindset and all of these characteristics in Jesus. This is how He viewed power, possessions, position, prestige, and productivity.

AVOID FALSE HUMILITY

Do not assume that humility requires you to abandon whatever authority and power you've been given. You can exercise authority and power with both strength and humility, and there's no conflict between the two. It isn't arrogant to be strong. Jesus calls us to meekness, but meekness is not weakness. Meekness is willful restraint. It's strength under control of a higher value and purpose. It's Jesus choosing not to call down a legion of angels to deliver Him. Being a servant does not imply being passive, disengaged, or weak.

Also do not assume that humility means saying no to the opportunities you're given, even if you feel unqualified, undeserving, or uncomfortable with the confidence or admiration people are giving you. I've seen many people back away from what God called them to do because they didn't want to assume too much or act in pride. The world desperately needs Christians who will be strong, bold, and courageous in humbly using their platforms to be a positive, kingdom-oriented influence.

At times I've been reluctant to say yes when invited to go places and serve in leadership positions because I didn't see myself in those circles. I tried to excuse myself from the request with a humble, "I'm just a guy who teaches the Bible." But in truth, it was false humility. In reality, I didn't want to deal with the weight and pressure that I knew would come with assuming greater leadership responsibility. It had nothing to do with humility. I had to be honest with myself and step up and step out. There is nothing arrogant or presumptuous about recognizing the resources God has given you—positions, possessions, power, or anything else—and humbly stewarding them.

Love is giving other people what they need the most when they deserve it the least, often at great personal cost.

True greatness starts with a mindset that neither prioritizes nor rejects the outward signs of success but instead approaches all people and situations with humility. It will cost you something, but not nearly as much as it cost Jesus to descend from heaven because of His love for us. We can hardly grasp how the God worshiped by all of creation took on human flesh to come live in filth and deal with the corruption, abuses, and rejection of this world. He was beaten, stripped in front of the very people He created, and hammered to a cross to experience excruciating pain, and His Father turned His back as He bore our sins. That's the greatest act of love and humility the world will ever know.

Love is giving other people what they need the most when they deserve it the least, often at great personal cost. You can't do it without humility. According to Jesus, Paul, and the testimony of Scripture, that's the path to *true* greatness.

HIGH COST, HIGH REWARD

At times we emphasize the cost and challenges of following Jesus' way to greatness without giving equal thought to the amazing rewards. The cost may be high, but the reward of true greatness when we follow Jesus' example of servanthood is beyond measure. What the Father did for the Son, He will do for you.

So, what did the Father do for the Son? What was Christ's reward for humbling Himself, becoming a bondservant, and offering Himself up in sacrifice?

> God *highly exalted* Him, and bestowed on Him the *name which is above every name*, so that at the name of Jesus every knee will bow, of those who are in heaven and on earth and under the earth, and that every tongue will confess that Jesus Christ is Lord, to the glory of God the Father. (Phil. 2:9–11, italics added)

The language here is superlative. It literally says God "super-exalted" Jesus. He bestowed on Jesus the name that is above every other name. Every knee of every creature in heaven, earth, and under the earth—all who love and trust Him, all who have rebelled against Him, and all who deny He exists—will bow to Him and confess that He is Lord.

This is the supreme example of a biblical principle that applies to every single one of us: God exalts the humble.

If you live in humility, God will lift you up at the proper time. It doesn't even matter how you got there—whether you've willingly humbled yourself as a spiritual choice, experienced His overwhelming grace and goodness and felt unworthy, been crushed with a devastating disease or circumstance, been betrayed or abused by people you trusted, been brought low because of a bad decision or your own sin, or any other reason. When broken, hurting, repentant people cry out to God in their desperation and ask for forgiveness and restoration, even when they are suffering from their own willful pride and rebellion and think God would never listen to them, He steps in. Scripture assures us again and again that He is near to the brokenhearted and saves those with a contrite spirit.

James wrote about this principle in his letter too: "Humble yourselves in the presence of the Lord, and He will exalt you" (James 4:10). He even walks us through the process: Resist the devil, and he will flee; draw near to God, and he will draw near to you; cleanse your hands and purify your heart; and humble yourself under God's mighty hand (James 4:7–10). God's response is to exalt you. He lifts up those who bow down.

God wants you to be a trophy of His grace.

God wants you to be a trophy of His grace. He wants to glorify His sons and daughters in a way that they reflect His glory. He may even want you to be famous. But He will want that fame to rest primarily on His character displayed in you. The highest compliments a person can receive are relational: "The most loving person I've ever met . . . the most generous businessperson I know . . . so sensitive to other people's needs . . . so courageous and kind . . . genuinely accepting of people who are far from God . . ." People are praised and affirmed when they reflect the nature of God.

This is the greatness God especially loves to see, and one way or another, He will lift up those who humble themselves before Him. He may lift each of us up in different ways, but He will honor those who honor Him.

Jesus became famous for the glory of God. He paid a terrible price, but He was motivated by the joy set before Him (Heb. 12:2). He saw the end of the story. If you are humble, you will probably have to endure some painful, unjust situations in this life. If you're generous, someone may take advantage of you. If you're loving, someone may always take it in and never give it back. But God will exalt you. You may be brought low for a moment, but keep your eye on how it all ends. He lifts you up for eternity. His rewards are real and never-ending.

Don't make the mistake of thinking everyone gets the same thing in heaven. God says He will reward different people in different ways. You get in by grace alone, but Jesus taught about rewards often, and so did Paul. Our salvation is by grace through faith, but we are rewarded according to our faithfulness. And the greatest reward is meeting Jesus, living in the new heaven and new earth, and experiencing God's goodness forever and ever.

You can endure a lot of difficulties when you focus on that reward. Paul suffered a lot, but as he neared the end of his earthly race, he looked forward to the reward laid up for him and for all those who look forward to Jesus' appearing (2 Tim. 4:8). Humble, sacrificial servanthood is a small price to pay in light of the magnificence of what God has in store for us. Putting everything on the altar to surrender to Him as Lord—your dreams, priorities, relationships, money, possessions, reputation, and even your own life—is a very worthwhile exchange. You will never regret it.

The truth is that everyone is going to bow the knee before Jesus and recognize Him as King of kings and Lord of lords.

The truth is that everyone is going to bow the knee before Jesus and recognize Him as King of kings and Lord of lords. Now is a much better time to do that than later. If Jesus is who He said He is and did what Scripture says He did, and you believe He is your

Savior, the only logical response—your reasonable service of worship (Rom. 12:1)—is to go all in. I think most Christians believe in Jesus and follow Him, but only as long as He doesn't ask too much, expect them to relocate, rearrange their dreams and desires, and expect costly sacrifices. But that's not how it works. If He is Lord, we offer Him *everything*. And humbly submitting to that truth will lead to exaltation and great rewards. You give up control, but you gain God's richest eternal blessings.

If you embrace this example of Jesus and make it your model for life, over time you will become the kind of Christian that your kids and grandkids, friends and neighbors, coworkers and fellow church members will remember as a great person. I've done a lot of funerals, and I've never heard people sit around and talk about the deceased in terms of how much jewelry they had, what kind of car they drove, how much money they threw around, or any other superficial characteristic. People remember how much a person loved others, how kind they were, what sort of influence they had, and whose lives they touched. Humility is the pathway to becoming the greatest person you can be, and that person is someone who serves and loves well.

GOD WANTS YOU TO BE GREAT!

God has great plans for you. He wants you to be great—a great Christian; a great mom or dad; a great employer, employee, or student; and a great member of your church and community. He doesn't want you to settle for being average or kind of good. He really does encourage your desire to make a difference with your life, use your gifts and talents to their fullest, and be *great* in His eyes. And He's pointing to Jesus and saying, "Here's how you get there. Descend into your greatness."

Remember the key steps in that journey:

- *The acid test of greatness is love.*
- *The road to greatness is humility.*
- *The opportunity for greatness is serving.*

Start where you are. Even little steps make a huge difference and can begin to shift your mindset. Here are some suggestions for putting these principles into practice:

- *Serve your church.* It doesn't have to be a huge commitment. Serve once a month in the nursery or welcoming people who come through the doors. Help clean up a room or two after the service. You don't even have to take the lead on this. Just be willing to support the people and ministries of your church.
- *Use your gifts.* Most church leaders are longing for people who will get involved and solve big problems with the various gifts and skills they've been given.
- *Show that you care.* Look around at all the people in our world who are wounded, hurting, and silently crying out for meaning and purpose. Even small expressions of love and compassion go a long way toward healing hearts and imparting the grace of God. Kind words and reassuring smiles are hardly sacrifices, but they mean a lot. Sometimes they even draw people to Jesus. Share them freely.
- *Be a thoughtful, kind coworker.* You'll spend most of your waking hours at work. Refuse to compartmentalize your faith. Be that coworker who thinks of others, affirms others, helps them celebrate the success of others, and does your job with excellence and integrity for an audience of One (Col. 3:23).
- *Offer yourself.* Hanging on the wall of my home office is the Prayer of St. Francis, and I pray it a lot. It beautifully articulates

the mindset of Jesus in offering Himself to us. As you learn to embrace this mindset for yourself, I'd encourage you to copy it, put it somewhere visible, and pray it often too:

Lord, make me an instrument of Your peace:
where there is hatred, let me sow love;
where there is injury, pardon;
where there is doubt, faith;
where there is despair, hope;
where there is darkness, light;
where there is sadness, joy.

O divine Master, grant that I may not so much seek
to be consoled as to console,
to be understood as to understand,
to be loved as to love.
For it is in giving that we receive,
it is in pardoning that we are pardoned,
and it is in dying that we are born to eternal life.

Believe it or not, God wants you to experience exceeding joy. This is your calling and your birthright as His child. He is pointing the way through the incarnation of Jesus. A life of humble sacrifice and service may sound unexciting, but it's incredibly fulfilling. Whatever love and grace you pour into other people, it will be poured back into you. God will make sure of it.

QUESTIONS FOR REFLECTION/DISCUSSION

1. What struck you in the opening story of this chapter about the wealthy, powerful executives?

2. Take a moment and think through how Jesus' humility redefined how to view the following measurements of success from Philippians 2 and how you can do the same:

- Power & Possessions = See them as gifts to steward, not control.
- Position & Prestige = Live for God's approval, not men's.
- Productivity = Success is accomplishing God's will.

3. What fears do you have of following Jesus' example? What do you fear you will miss out on?

4. What specific next steps would God have you take to develop a servant's heart and mind?

5. How can you embrace and steward the power, possessions, position, prestige, and productivity the Lord has allowed you to attain?

Part 3: Love Obeys

Whoever has my commands and keeps them
is the one who loves me. The one who loves me
will be loved by my Father, and I too will love
them and show myself to them. . . .
Anyone who loves me will obey my teaching.
My Father will love them, and we will come
to them and make our home with them.

John 14:21, 23 NIV

CHAPTER 5

Love Obeys

Theresa and I had been married about a week, maybe even less. We returned home from our honeymoon and were ready to start our new life together. Apparently, each of us had some expectations about what that life would look like that were not rooted in reality.

In my family, breakfast had always been a big deal. Sometime before 6:30, I could hear bacon and eggs sizzling in the pan and my mom singing along with the radio. It didn't matter what time I had to leave for school; we would sit down at the table at 6:30 and have a full-blown breakfast. We were a morning family, and this was our normal way of life. I didn't know anything different.

If Theresa and I had had premarital counseling, I don't think that would have come up. I didn't think it was even a question. This is just what people did. Breakfast really matters to me, and I assumed that when I woke up in the morning, it would be there for me.

The first morning of living in our new home together, I didn't smell any bacon, so I asked, "What's for breakfast?"

"Well," she said, "there's milk in the refrigerator and cereal in the pantry."

Theresa has always prepared great food and been a great homemaker, but the full home-cooked breakfast (bacon, eggs, and toast) I thought would be part of my future never materialized except on very special occasions. That just wasn't her thing.

On the other hand, Theresa grew up with a father who could fix almost anything. He knew how to change the oil, clean out a carburetor, and do all kinds of handyman jobs around the house. I don't even know where a carburetor is. I never learned to change the oil myself until college when I was so broke that I had no other choice. But she assumed that I would take care of things like that because her father always had.

That's a relatively innocuous example, but like virtually any other married person on the planet, I could give plenty of others that have created more serious problems and pain. Our personal history is paramount in forming our expectations, and our expectations powerfully shape our relationships and our responses to them. Whatever we've learned from experience, we expect it to apply in the future. We tend to apply to our current relationships whatever our past relationships have trained us to believe.

> **Our faith, our conversations with God, and our thoughts about the future are all shaped by the expectations we've developed.**

If this is true of our relationships with people, just think of how true it is in our relationship with God. We have unconscious expectations about who He is, what He does, and how He will work in our lives. How do we expect Him to show up in certain situations? How does He take care of us? What can we trust Him to do? Which prayers can we trust Him to answer? Our faith, our conversations with Him, and our thoughts about the future are all shaped by the expectations we've developed.

We can also flip that question around. What does God expect of us? You may have grown up in a faith tradition or no tradition at all. Your relationships with other Christians and the teachings you've heard have shaped your perspectives on what He expects of you. Here, too, history always influences our expectations.

Two Critical Question

- What can I expect from God?
- What does God expect from me?

In the first two chapters, we saw that *love gives*. Humble people have a worldview that says, "I am second." When we give our time, attention, help, resources, or friendship in love, that's a sign of humility. We are putting other people ahead of ourselves.

In the next two chapters, we saw that *love serves*. This also flows out of a worldview of humility. We learn to put away our pride and serve people. It takes practice, but it's part of becoming a more loving Christian.

In this chapter and the next, we will see how *love obeys*. And the way it obeys has a lot to do with how we answer these two questions about our expectations in our relationship with God—what we expect of Him, and what He expects of us. All of us bring a personal history into that relationship, and because our experience is so complex and nuanced—deeply spiritual, psychological, relational, and emotional—most of our expectations are unconscious.

TWO VIEWS ON EXPECTATIONS WITH GOD

Not only does our personal history shape our expectations of God and our understanding of His expectations for us. So does church history. And historically, people have answered these two questions in two main ways that are very, very different from each other.

In answering the first question—what can we expect from God—some people assume that if you believe in Jesus and live faithfully, you can expect health, wealth, wisdom, strong relationships, and a life primarily full of blessings. You may go through some occasional adversity, but you'll come through it in great shape. This view represents what often is called the "prosperity gospel." Since God is good, He wants to bless us, and it is our lack of faith or disobedience that explains why we might not be experiencing bigger blessings. In this view, if you're right with God, "life will be awesome." Unfortunately, this teaching can lead to false guilt or becoming disillusioned. When life for whatever reason turns out to be anything but awesome, those holding this view are prone to quit, believing they must have done something wrong, or worse, assuming God doesn't keep His promises, if He exists at all!

Unfortunately, this teaching can lead to false guilt or becoming disillusioned.

At the other end of the spectrum, some people assume that your faith in Jesus assures you of being loved and forgiven by God, but you can't take anything else for granted. Suffering, pain, injustice, adversity are simply reflections of the normal Christian life. Jesus went to the cross and called us to follow Him, so we can expect a difficult and demanding life of suffering. This view sees God as generally benevolent, all-powerful, and somewhat distant like the hard-to-please parent who is saving most of the blessings for heaven, not here on earth. He is holy, but we are unworthy and must work hard to live up to His high expectations. These people may struggle with guilt whenever they experience something good, because they know they aren't worthy of it and they don't expect God to indulge us very much.

These are both extreme caricatures—most people fall somewhere in between and blend these perspectives—but you get the point. People generally lean in one direction or the other in their assumptions about what to expect from God. The truth is God is good, kind, and generous and longs to bless us. And we are called to take up our cross and follow Him out of love and loyalty. In a world that is fallen, energized by Satan, and bombarding us with temptation, suffering and trouble will certainly be part of our story; but not because God is hard to please or doesn't care about us.

The second question comes with a more formal theological history, and this is where answers diverge into two very distinct categories. Both can be supported biblically, to a point, but both tend to go beyond biblical teaching in developing a system of thought through which the Scripture is interpreted.

I'll acknowledge up front that my descriptions of these two main theological camps will overgeneralize their positions. Adherents of each side could read this and think, *That's not what we believe!* I realize this is not a full presentation of their doctrines. But because this book is not a systematic theology and cannot go into all the depth and nuances of these rich theological traditions, I'll present them both in broad brushstrokes. These are the general positions at the polar extremes. Just know that things are a good bit more complex than I'm suggesting. In fact, what I'm presenting is not so much these traditions as their founders would express them, but how these positions get characterized by well-meaning adherents of both camps.

THE CALVINIST ANSWERS

John Calvin was a sixteenth-century Swiss theologian whose writings and teachings were extremely influential. He was brilliant in his analysis and he profoundly shaped the Protestant Reformation. What we call Calvinism today has developed from his insights, though many of his positions have been pushed into formulations that he might not have fully embraced.

Calvin emphasized God's sovereignty in our salvation. He thoroughly explored the biblical idea of predestination (Rom. 8:30; Eph. 1:4–5) to the neglect (in the view of some) of a human responsibility to repent and exercise faith for salvation. In extreme Calvinism, God already knows who will be saved and who won't be, and even more, He has already *determined* who will be saved and who won't be. So any response to Christ, whether positive or negative, has already been known and predestined. You believe what you believe because God ordained it, not because you chose it, even if from your own perspective you made the decision.

So when we come to Philippians 2:12–13, for example, Calvin would emphasize Paul's statement that "it is God who is at work in you, both to will and to work for His good pleasure." God's work in the individual, not the individual's response, is the key factor. And because salvation and perseverance in faith are works of God, a believer is eternally secure. Since God has perfect foreknowledge, He doesn't begin a work in someone and then abandon it because it isn't going well. If He begins a work in a person, He will complete it, and there's nothing the person can do to forfeit the grace God has already given.

Most Christians have been shaped by some aspects of this system of thought to some degree. Presbyterians, most Anglicans, many

Baptists, many Bible churches, and a number of other denominational streams come out of this Reformed tradition.

THE ARMINIAN ANSWERS

About eighty years after Calvin, a man named Jacob Arminius, in response to some of the extreme Calvinistic teaching, argued that Calvinism (primarily as taught by Calvin's followers) did not align with biblical revelation. Even though it drew from biblical principles, it organized them in a way that didn't reflect the whole truth.

Arminius emphasized human responsibility and free will over Calvin's emphasis on God's sovereignty. He believed in God's sovereign rule in the universe, of course, but did not believe God usurped human choices in receiving salvation by faith. Where Calvin focused on God at work in the individual, Arminius focused on the last phrase in the preceding verse: "work out your salvation with fear and trembling" (Phil. 2:12). He believed that people who lose their faith *can* lose their salvation. God respects the will of human beings so much that He lets their eternal destiny depend on it.

Denominations that come out of the Arminian tradition include Wesleyans (Methodists, Nazarenes), most Pentecostal and charismatic groups, and Church of Christ and Disciples of Christ, among others.

CHURCH HISTORY—TWO VIEWS CONCERNING GOD'S EXPECTATIONS

The chart and summary below is how these two traditions have often been oversimplified, characterized, and then weaponized in relationships within the Christian church.

CALVIN	ARMINIUS
Sovereignty	Responsibility
Predestination	Free Will
"It's God who's at work"	"Work out your salvation"
"Whatever will be, will be"	Choices have consequences
Eternally Secure	Eternally Uncertain
"Let go, and let God"	"Let's go and let's get with it!"

Over the centuries, the well-defined views of some Calvinist and Arminian denominations have morphed into more accommodating, less dogmatic positions, such that many churches don't hold the beliefs of their founding movements as strongly as they once did. My point is not to come down on one side or the other or to critique either of these streams of thought. I'm simply suggesting that each one, taken to an extreme, can lead to some false expectations and errors in how we live out the Christian life.

If you so strongly emphasize God's sovereignty that you neglect human responsibility, for example, you might assume your entire life that God is accomplishing His purposes in you when in fact He is calling you to participate very actively in those purposes. Or, if you have sinned terribly and are filled with anxiety about the status of your salvation, you may be consumed with overwhelming guilt and never experience the promise and peace of God's grace.

I believe the Bible holds both of these views in tension. Acts 13:48, for example, says, "As many as had been appointed to eternal life believed." But only a few verses later, it says Paul's preaching was so persuasive that many trusted Christ (Acts 14:1). Which is it? Appointed to eternal life or persuaded to believe? Both are biblically true.

Let me give you an example that has been very helpful for me.

When I was in seminary, I had a professor who clearly and brilliantly explained complex theological concepts. His name was Dr. Charles Ryrie, and many people today still use Bibles with his name on the cover and his notes in the margins. I took many of my theology classes from him. He was very thin and wore wire-rimmed glasses, and he would put his hands behind his back and barely move an inch from behind the lectern. He was not a dynamic, inspirational communicator, but he was so crystal clear with his logic, exegesis, and word choice that he captivated our attention.

One day Dr. Ryrie said, "Gentlemen [almost all seminary students were men then], make sure you are here today and our next class period. You cannot miss either one. I'm going to take the Calvinist position today, and the Arminian position tomorrow." And he proceeded to explain Calvinist thought point by point, passage by passage, with ample biblical evidence and plain, irrefutable logic. I left class thinking no one could ever argue with that. It was airtight.

The next class, he went through the Arminian position point by point, passage by passage, with ample biblical evidence and plain, irrefutable logic. I left class thinking no one could ever argue with that either. It was equally airtight.

When he was finished, he said, "These are great men of God who, in their period of history, were responding to different things. Now imagine a telephone pole, and imagine the guide wires attached to it. One goes in this direction; one goes in the opposite direction. The Bible teaches that God is absolutely and totally sovereign. It also teaches that we are fully and completely responsible. Just like the tension that holds that pole, those truths are the tension that holds each side of our relationship with God."

Then he said, "When you read the Bible, be a biblicist, not someone who buys into a system." The question to the answer is always: What does the text say?

I used to save all my hardest questions for Howard Hendricks, another of my professors, and I remember his response when I asked him about this one. "Chip, why would you expect a finite person like me to explain an infinite God and the mystery of His wisdom? Read the text. When it says He's sovereign and He chooses, it means He's sovereign and He chooses. When it says whosoever believes, it means whosoever believes. I don't know how it all works, but I don't have to. He does." The Scripture is our final authority!

The question to the answer is always: What does the text say?

I have a high view of theology, but I've learned from multiple perspectives, and I'm convinced that when we choose one biblical view to the exclusion of all others, we end up in error. As Dr. Ryrie masterfully pointed out, we like to have a system and then find passages that support that system, overlooking other passages that don't.

The Bible presents a fuller truth. It rejects both extremes and holds God's sovereignty and human responsibility in "biblical tension" and balance. The sovereignty of our all-knowing, all-powerful God and the responsibility of human beings stand in dynamic tension, and we have to affirm both.

Now all of that is a preface to our discussion of a beautiful passage in Philippians 2 that, on the surface, may seem contradictory. But it's one of those passages we have to look at and say, "Both of these things are true."

SOVEREIGNTY AND RESPONSIBILITY IN HARMONY

We first went through verses 1–4 and learned that we are to live in humble, loving unity and consider others more important than ourselves. Then in verses 5–11, we explored the "Christ hymn," that majestic and mysterious passage about Jesus' descent to earth in the incarnation and His exaltation above all things in heaven and earth, and learned that we are to have the same mindset that Jesus had. Now in verse 12, which I referred to briefly above, we learn that love not only *gives* and *serves*, it also *obeys*.

> So then, my beloved, just as you have always obeyed, not as in my presence only, but now much more in my absence, work out your salvation with fear and trembling; for it is God who is at work in you, both to will and to work for His good pleasure. (Phil. 2:12–13)

Remember, Paul is writing to Christians about unity in the church. He isn't in Philippi, so he can't speak directly to the conflict that is growing between two prominent women. He does know these believers are struggling with persecution and wondering why they are suffering, to which Paul suggests they should consider suffering a privilege and a gift. They are being opposed, just as Jesus and Paul were opposed (Phil. 1:29–30). It's normal. These external and internal pressures are the context for these verses.

So, in light of this disunity problem, which at its heart is a love and humility problem, here's what he wants them to do: *obey*, just as they had in the past when he was there with them.

The command Paul gives them is interesting and also a little confusing for people who know we are saved by grace through faith alone. "Work out your salvation with fear and trembling," he tells them. If we didn't know better, we might think Paul is contradicting his own message and telling these people to earn their salvation through their works.

That's not what he means, of course. Paul is actually using mining language here, urging them to work out their claim, to mine the riches they have already been given. A mine full of gold doesn't do you any good unless you start digging and extract the gold.

Our salvation is like a gold mine. I could hand you a Bible and say, "All the truth you need to live a godly, fulfilling, abundant life is in this book," but if you just set it on your shelf and never opened it, you wouldn't benefit from it. You could go through life not knowing what to do in certain situations, how to be a good spouse or parent, how to handle your money in God-honoring ways, or what to think about the future of the world, all while the riches of God's wisdom lay on your bookshelf. You'd *have* the truth, but you haven't *accessed* the truth.

In this passage, the Philippians' salvation isn't in question, but what they get out of it is. So Paul wants them to get the most out of the eternal gift God has given them, and he says to do it with fear and trembling—reverential awe. Your salvation will get you to heaven, but all its treasures for here and now remain hidden if you don't know how to apply them. We need to work out what God has worked in.

That's the responsibility side of the equation. In the next verse,

Paul gives us the reason: "For it is God who is at work in you, both to will and to work for His good pleasure."

The word for "work" in this verse (but not the previous verse) is the same word we get "energy" from. Whenever this word is used in the New Testament, it refers to God's power, not ours. Paul also uses it in Ephesians 3:20 when he says God is able to do exceedingly beyond what we can ask or think according to the power *working* within us.

When this was used in early Greek, long before the New Testament, it referred to the inner character of someone who had performed a heroic deed. It was the internal source of courageous deeds. It literally means "effective action." What Paul is saying, then, is that God's power is effectively working within us to produce change—not as an external pressure but as a transformation generated from within. And it always achieves its desired result.

That's the sovereignty side of the equation. God is doing it. We participate in it, but He is the source of power. He is initiating the work. Grace is a gift from Him. In fact, that's the overall message of the book of Galatians—that just as we are saved by grace through faith, we are sanctified by grace through faith. We live out the Christian life the same way we received it.

If I could paraphrase Paul in these two verses, here's how I would say it: "Philippians, in light of your situation, and in light of the mindset Jesus modeled for us, even though I'm not there with you, I want you to *obey* as if I were. And here's what I want you to do: Work out the grace that God has worked into you. Treat each other with humility. Forgive each other. Resolve this rift. If you don't think you can, think again. God is working into you His will and His power to do it for His own good pleasure."

When we take a step of faith and obedience, we find all the grace and power we need to fulfill what God wants us to do. It's already there. We need to extract it, but it is He who has worked it into us.

Do you see the two sides coming together? God's sovereignty, human responsibility, all woven together.

> **When we take a step of faith and obedience, we find all the grace and power we need to fulfill what God wants us to do.**

So, becoming like Jesus and following Him is a cooperative effort—our effort and discipline not to earn but to mine the depths of the grace that God has given us.

This was the passage that finally helped me put the Calvinist-Arminian divide in perspective. I clearly saw both God's sovereignty and human responsibility in it, right there in two parts of the same sentence.

There have been times in church history when people have pressed these positions so far into the extremes that they ended up with really distorted doctrines—like "double predestination," in which God not only ordains who is going to heaven but also who is going to hell. At the height of this controversy during and after the Reformation, some people would give a testimony of how they realized that they had been chosen to go to hell for the glory of God. At the other extreme, some walk on eggshells their entire lives because they are afraid they will mess up once and lose their salvation or miss an opportunity to share Christ with someone and be responsible for that person's eternity in hell.

I've known people who struggle mightily with guilt because no matter how much they do, it's never enough. They are living hyper-responsible lives, as though God has placed everything on their shoulders. I've also known people who are so laid-back that they aren't even living out their calling because "God is in control." It's true that He is in control, but that doesn't excuse someone from obeying what He commands. Both of these extremes are distortions of truth.

I've been around smart people who are fully convinced that the Calvinist or Arminian position is *the* scriptural truth and the other side is completely in error, and sometimes these smart people can be very intimidating. I finally had to realize that it wasn't up to me to explain everything. I can clearly see God's sovereignty and human responsibility and free will in Scripture.

Are our prayers predetermined? When James writes, "You have not because you ask not," there is unmistakable contingency in those words. When I praise God, is that from my own heart or is God just pulling the strings of His little puppet? It has to be freely given to be genuine. But I also take great comfort in God's sovereignty, because if everything depends on me, I can't handle the weight of it.

Eventually I began to see both principles everywhere. In Philippians 1, Paul expressed confidence that he would be delivered through the provision of the Spirit of Jesus (sovereignty) and through the Philippians' prayers (responsibility). In chapter 2, God desires unity for His people and will work it into them (sovereignty), but it isn't going to happen if they don't make some choices about their attitudes and perspectives (responsibility). And here in Philippians 2:12–13, the Philippians need to mine the riches of their salvation (responsibility), but it is God willing and working within them for His good pleasure (sovereignty).

Fortunately, more and more churches are recognizing the best of both positions and focusing more on letting the Bible have its tensions without having to systematize truth into a fully explainable whole.

To be clear, there are significant differences, and people still debate these issues. Coherent theology and doctrine are important. But divides like these are not worth splitting our fellowship, which has happened countless times in church history. In fact, Paul's words about unity in Philippians 2 would resolve a lot of tension between rival theological camps. Scripture never tells us to agree on everything. It does tell us to love one another in humility.

That's the continuing theme throughout this chapter of Philippians, and now that Paul has presented the principles, he is going to get even more specific about how to carry them out. The attitudes that go with love, humility, servanthood, and unity not only build up the fellowship in the Spirit of Jesus, they also demonstrate His love and power to a watching world.

Scripture never tells us to agree on everything. It does tell us to love one another in humility.

This chapter may feel like we took a detour on our journey to become more loving people, to choose love in every circumstance. But I assure you, much of our lack of obedience and, therefore, lack of love is rooted in deep seated and often unconscious perspectives of what we can expect from God and what He indeed expects from us. I encourage you to take some time right now and ponder the questions below. God longs for you to flourish in your relationships, which requires getting below the surface and examining your view of God and how you assume He views you.

QUESTIONS FOR REFLECTION/DISCUSSION

1. What conscious or unconscious expectations have you had of God and His role in your life?

2. What conscious or unconscious expectations have you believed God has of you?

3. What is God's part in our ongoing transformation to become like Jesus? What's our part?

4. What new insight did you get from this chapter? Who might you encourage with what you learned?

CHAPTER 6

Working Out What God Worked In

The Philippian believers had opponents and were apparently intimidated by them.

Paul referred to the "suffering" and "conflict" they endured as a small religious minority in a city full of imperial worship and polytheism and urged this church to stand firm (Phil. 1:28–30). In a Roman colony like Philippi, Jewish and Christian beliefs were considered strange religions from the east, and, as in many Roman cities, those who refused to make sacrifices to the emperor could be seen as a threat to political and social stability. Paul had discovered the same thing the first time he visited Philippi, as the business community accused these "Jews" of promoting unlawful customs (Acts 16:20–21). It wasn't easy to be a follower of Jesus there.

The Philippians were not facing severe persecution, necessarily. Paul never refers to any threats of violence or imprisonment. But constant pressure and scorn are hard to endure, especially in the marketplace and civic life, and the Philippian Christians suffered under the strain. So, Paul now turns to their testimony as lights "in the midst of a crooked and perverse generation" (Phil. 2:15). The "cancel culture" is not new and Philippians 2:14–18 provides God's specific instruction on how to respond.

How were they to conduct themselves in this hostile environment? How should they work out what God has worked into their lives? How should citizens of God's kingdom live among citizens of imperial Rome? In light of the principles he has just given them, he gives them several very practical things to *obey* that will give them a shining testimony in a dark world.

THE COMMAND: BE A GRATEFUL SERVANT

Paul has told us to mine the riches of our salvation in Christ. What does that look like? What is our responsibility as believers in Jesus in light of what the sovereign God has done in our life? Paul's answers to those questions have crucial implications for the pressures the Philippians were facing and similar ones we face today. For the sake of internal unity and external witness, every believer should live as a grateful servant.

> Do all things without grumbling or disputing; so that you will prove yourselves to be blameless and innocent, children of God above reproach in the midst of a crooked and perverse generation, among whom you appear as lights in the world, holding fast the word of life. (Phil. 2:14–16)

Notice how comprehensive this overarching command is: Do *everything* without grumbling or disputing. This is the third time Paul has issued a strong command in Philippians 2. The first two were in verses 3–4, where he says to do nothing from selfishness or pride and not to look out for our self-interests. This one is just as decisive. Whatever situation these believers find themselves in, no matter how unfair or oppressive they think it is, whatever pushback or hostility they have to endure, they are to engage each other and their community without any complaining or arguing.

The word for "grumbling" implies negativity, pessimism, having a bad attitude toward whatever a person is going through. Together, these words reflect infectious negative attitudes. We are to be grateful servants in our thoughts and words—no whining, sarcasm, criticism, contempt, insults, gossip, or tearing anyone down. It's a very convicting standard.

The word for "disputing" here is a legal term referring to the kind of arguments one might make in a court case. It also implies being provocative, contentious, or divisive. Paul sees the potentially damaging effects of factionalism, of taking sides in a dispute, not only in Philippi but among all believers everywhere, and wants Christian relationships to be free from that kind of dissension. It's easy to get sucked into a culture of contentiousness, name-calling, snarky comebacks, complaints about whatever raw deal we've been given, and criticism of what other people are doing—especially in an age of social media—but that culture is toxic. We are called to live above it.

The words Paul chooses here are not nearly as surprising as the way he arranges them. He places "all things" right at the beginning of the sentence to emphasize how comprehensive he means for this command to be, as if to say, "Yes, I know people aren't treating you fairly. I know you live in a hostile environment. But there are no exceptions here. In all of your circumstances, relationships, and activities—whether fair or not, whether in your fellowship or in your community—your testimony depends on your attitude."

Think of all the ways that applies to your life. "All things" includes managing your workload, driving on the expressway, paying your taxes, having to contact customer service, interacting with people at stores and restaurants, dealing with a difficult client or family member, living with your spouse, and on and on. It's all-inclusive.

Then Paul ties this command to a very specific purpose: that this fellowship of believers would appear as blameless, pure, faultless children of God—bright lights in a dark night. His instructions will certainly strengthen their relationships with each other, but he has a bigger picture in mind. He wants them to make an impression on the world around them.

Because Philippi was a Roman colony with a lot of ties to Rome and special status for many of its citizens, its laws and customs reflected Roman values and ways. The city prided itself on its Roman-ness and its connections with the imperial center. That wasn't going to change, least of all through any criticism from a marginal sect. Followers of Jesus had nothing to gain by lamenting their status, critiquing the dominant culture, or arguing for their own rights. In fact, that would undermine their message.

So, let me ask you, how are you doing with not grumbling, complaining, criticizing, or tearing down others in your family? Church? Work? If I logged on to the last six months of your social media posts, or things you've forwarded to friends, would you be a shining light or adding to the darkness? Reversing the toxic culture in our world of division over politics and differences of opinion and values has to start with us.

THE PURPOSE: BE A GODLY SERVANT

Instead, they were to "prove themselves" to be blameless, innocent, and above reproach—or, as some translations put it, "pure" and "faultless." In all, Paul uses three Greek words that have something to do with personal purity. "Blameless" means to be above reproach with the outside world, not giving Christianity a bad name. No one should be able to point to you and wonder what kind of person would claim a message of love and "good news" and then post something like that, treat a cashier or server that way, use that kind of language, have such questionable morals, or live without love, hope, or joy. Whether you have a fish on the back of your car is not the point; Christians need to have a solid reputation that demonstrates the character of Jesus. "Blameless" means consistently choosing not to live in a way that reflects negatively on Jesus and His people.

Christians need to have a solid reputation that demonstrates the character of Jesus.

"Innocent children of God" refers to personal purity. The word is often used of a metal and the level of impurities mixed into it. Applied spiritually, this kind of purity is holistic: pure in thoughts and attitudes toward other people; pure in personal goals and agendas; morally, ethically, and sexually pure; and in all ways living a holy, set-apart life.

The third word, "above reproach" or "without fault," does not imply perfection. Otherwise Paul would be giving an impossible command. This term is often used in relation to God and bringing an offering to Him. Jewish law forbade sacrificing a sick or blemished lamb as an offering to God because that wasn't really a sacrifice. We are to offer God our best, which includes offering Him lives that reflect the work of grace He has done in us (Rom. 12:1).

These descriptive words express the kind of testimony we are to have in "a crooked and perverse generation." "Crooked" is the word from which we get "scoliosis," a curvature of the spine. "Perverse" means twisted or degenerate. Paul is well aware that the Philippians (along with all Christians in all times and places) were living in a world that has twisted things around. This world has moral scoliosis. It has taken everything God has given us to flourish—life, truth, morality, relationships, and resources—and distorted them, turning them toward selfish and ungodly purposes.

Imagine what grumbling, complaining, and arguing would accomplish in that kind of environment. If Christian attitudes blend in with the character and mood of a fallen, twisted world, who is left to demonstrate an alternative? How can people living in darkness ever see the light if no one is shining? "If the salt loses its saltiness," according to Jesus, "it is no longer good for anything" (Matt. 5:13 NIV). That's the purpose behind being a grateful and godly servant—living in a way that presents a clear alternative for people who have never known anything better than the corrupt, contentious world they live in.

This is an extremely high calling, isn't it? It might be tempting to read Paul's words here as a nice suggestion, a low-stakes encouragement to do better, if possible. But that isn't true at all. The stakes are very high. Our words, attitudes, and actions not only profoundly influence our own lives but also the people around us.

Our words reflect what's in our hearts, and our tongues are the rudders of our lives.

James wrote about this too—how essential it is to watch what comes out of our mouths (James 3:1–12). At the center of James's discussion of life transformation is this long section on the remarkable power of the tongue. Like a fire, it can burn down a forest, and like the rudder of a ship, it can send us off in one direction or another. Our words reflect what's in our hearts, and our tongues are the rudders of our lives, so if we want to change our lives, we need to change our words and the heart behind them. The course of our entire lives can be altered either positively or negatively by what comes out of our mouths. If we want anything about our lives to change, if we are serious about becoming loving people, we absolutely have to govern our speech.

That's essentially what Paul is telling the Philippians. Their entire testimony depends on gratitude rather than complaints coming out of their mouths.

I know a beautiful, godly young woman, who happens to be my daughter, who learned this lesson many years ago. Some kids look at life as a glass half full. Not Annie. She came out of the womb with a negative perspective. People who know her today can't even imagine this, but as a young girl, her words were negative almost all the time. I believe it came from the dark side of her gift of leadership—she was able to see what was wrong about a situation, which is a necessary gift for those who lead. But whatever she thought about a person or situation that needed correcting just came out of her mouth.

When Annie began having problems with friends at school, we went into training. She knew what Ephesians 4:29 said about not letting unwholesome words proceed from our mouths—Scripture memory had long been part of our family routine—so when something negative would come out of Annie's mouth, we'd say, "Annie, what does Ephesians 4:29 say?" Three minutes later, it would happen again.

So we set up a jar. With every unwholesome comment, she would have to put in a dime. She went through a lot of dimes. Then we upped it to a quarter. She went through a lot of those too. We decided everything in the jar would go to missions, so Annie became a great supporter of missionaries around the world.

This went on not for months but for a couple years, but eventually Annie became one of the most positive people you could ever meet. And I think she would agree that getting control of her tongue changed the course of her life.

One of the most vivid indicators that reveals where you are in your journey with the Lord is your speech. Your money is another one—your spending habits say a lot about your values—but what your speech says about your heart is just as telling. If you are in the habit of complaining, criticizing, or expressing other negative, unwholesome thoughts, your words need to change. Your speech and your heart are intricately connected. They each reflect the other. Change one, and the other will follow. "The good man out of the good treasure of his heart brings forth what is good; and the evil man out of the evil treasure brings forth what is evil; for his mouth speaks from that which fills his heart" (Luke 6:45).

One of the most vivid indicators that reveals where you are in your journey with the Lord is your speech.

Your testimony, not to mention your own well-being, depends on your words and attitudes. Paul's command to do everything without grumbling or disputing had a high-stakes purpose demonstrating the power of the gospel and the character of Jesus in a world that needs to know Him.

We can apply this today not only to the words that come out of our mouths but also through our fingertips. Watch what you post in the global community known as social media. Before you press "send," ask the Lord, "Is this what You want me to say?" If not, don't send it, no matter how angry you are. To be a godly servant, let everything be done, whether publicly, personally, or privately, without complaining, muttering, arguing, or being negative. Choosing to *obey* this command and intentionally going into training to govern your words will radically transform the love you give and the love you receive.

THE RESULT: BE A BOLD SERVANT

You and I both know that this is a process. You don't take a pill and suddenly become pure or blameless. It's a journey that takes you deeper and deeper into the character and nature of Christ. In order to be humble and servant-hearted with other believers and amid a skeptical or hostile world, you have to be proactive and have a plan. I call it spiritual training. Consider writing Ephesians 4:29 and Luke 6:45 on two separate 3x5 cards. On one side of each card write a brief sentence prayer—"Father, I want all my words to everyone, every day to honor You and express Your love. I ask you to make Ephesians 4:29 true in my life today." Then turn the card over and read the passage slowly, thoughtfully, and prayerfully. To start, do this when you get up and when you go to bed. Later you'll find yourself quoting it in the car, or silently in a meeting, or asking God to forgive you as your old speech habit will die hard. But you will see change and you can shine as a light in a dark world by what you say, and often by what you don't say. This is what it looks like to participate with the Spirit to work out what God has worked in.

But notice the result: We appear as lights in the world. You shine like a star.

That's what the world needs today. It doesn't need believers to prove we are right nearly as much as it needs us to demonstrate who we are in Christ. That hasn't happened to the extent it should have in the last few decades (or ever), which is why our message has gotten so lost in the midst of culture wars and social upheaval.

Working through media, education systems, political institutions, and other spheres of influence in our society is great, but it isn't enough. We've brought arguments to our world, when it really needs a display of Jesus.

When the church is godly, pure, bold, loving, and winsome, we shine a light into the world. When that light begins to fade, darkness grows, and it's an even darker darkness than before. According to Barna's research, more than 80 percent of those who claim to be Christian do not live any differently in their moral and ethical lives than non-Christians. They spend their money and raise their kids in about the same way, fudge on their taxes, gossip about people, get divorced at about the same rates, and generally hold similar values. I meet people across the country who say, "Christians are no different from the rest of us." And sadly, in many respects, they are right. It sounds so simple, but when Christians live like Christians, real change happens.

Statistics suggest that people who not only say they are Bible-believing followers of Jesus, but actually pray and read the Bible daily, live differently. But over time, much of the church has dumbed down the standards for what it means to live a holy, loving, radically committed life. There was a time when divorce, living together before marriage, pornography, and same-gender sexual relationships were considered unacceptable sins, but now many people consider those standards out of touch and irrelevant. I am amazed when I meet sincere, often churchgoing people who are shocked to learn that those behaviors are wrong. A fellow pastor who serves on his church's prayer team told me that a young couple came up asking for prayer about a big decision. They wanted him to pray for God's direction whether they should move in together. He kindly said they didn't even need to pray on that one, as God has made it clear in His Word. He shared God's wisdom and commands for a flourishing relationship (Eph. 5; 1 Thess. 4) and the role, timing, and reason for living apart. My point, obedience to the known will of God is the prerequisite and evidence for loving Jesus (John 14:21) and loving others well.

Don't get me wrong. God is a God of redemption and restoration. He forgives and restores lives from all kinds of sinful patterns and behaviors. But those patterns and behaviors should still be considered sinful. According to research by the Barna Group in partnership with Pure Desires Ministries, the statistics of men (including pastors) who indulge in or are addicted to pornography is alarming.[3] The number of churches that are abandoning biblical prohibitions against fornication, pornography, and homosexuality is staggering. Biblical principles that used to be taken for granted among believers are now matters of hot debate.

When we sow to the flesh, we reap corruption.

I'm not down on anyone who struggles with these things. Just the opposite—I want everyone to experience God's best for their lives. I know how sin and impurity can produce unhealthy, unwanted consequences. When we sow to the flesh, we reap corruption (Gal. 6:8). All of God's desires for us, which are expressed in His commands and instructions, are for our good and will lead to a life of flourishing. The Bible is not a legalistic handbook of regulations; it's a manual for life given to us by a loving God who knows that when we do life our way and not His, there will be painful consequences. "There is a way which seems right to a man, but its end is the way of death" (Prov. 14:12). He shares with us His divine wisdom so we can walk in His ways and experience the fullness of His blessings and joy.

Peter exhorted the early church to abandon their former lives of dysfunction and destruction in relationships. "As obedient children, do not be conformed to the former lusts which were yours in your ignorance, but like the Holy One who called you, be holy yourselves also in all your behavior; because it is written, 'YOU SHALL BE HOLY, FOR I AM HOLY'" (1 Peter 1:14–16). Anyone living a holy life today, even in the Christian community, is likely to be considered weird or legalistic. When we try to live up to God's standards in order to earn or merit salvation and a relationship with Him, that's legalism. But when we learn of His high standards and allow Him to empower us to live up to them, not to earn anything but to change inwardly, to love and honor Him, and experience His best for our lives, that's wisdom. And when we live out God's will for our lives, it reveals and magnifies who He is and what He's like to the world around us.

When we live out God's will for our lives, it reveals and magnifies who He is and what He's like to the world around us.

Much of what is called love today is lust. Love gives and wants what's best for the other; lust wants to get, to please oneself, and then it moves on when the excitement and infatuation wears off. The result: broken hearts and wounded lives. One of the most important decisions we can make is what we allow into our minds. We are the product of our thought life (Rom. 8:5–8); it shapes who we are and eventually comes out in our words and actions. This is why Paul says in another letter to set our minds on things above, not on things that are on earth, therefore putting aside all immorality, impurity, and evil desires (Col. 3:2, 5). We are transformed as our minds are renewed (Rom. 12:2). We are born of God's Spirit to live entirely new lives.

So, Paul says to be grateful, godly, and bold. Our gratitude and godliness have everything to do with our testimony as followers of Jesus—not by presenting an impossible standard to the people around us (which we can't live up to ourselves) but by authentically demonstrating that there's a better way than this darkened world understands.

Unfortunately, for many of us of an earlier generation, these commands for sexual purity and holy living came down to us as "laws against anything fun or pleasurable" from a distant, angry God. We got moralism and rules, but not the heart of God or the all-important *why* of these commands. In this next section, Paul wants these new Christians that he loves so much to understand *why* God gives these commands about speech and morality. His motive, far from any moralistic guilt trip, is something super positive that he doesn't want them to miss.

THE MOTIVE: BE A JOYFUL SERVANT

The motive behind the command, the purpose, and the result is one of the major themes of the entire letter: *Be joyful!*

All that Paul has said leading up to this passage—the love, unity, humility, and servant-heartedness he has called his readers to have, as well as the command to do all things without grumbling and disputing so they will appear as blameless lights in a dark world—is not a "have to" nearly as much as it's a "get to." Joy is behind it all.

> . . . so that in the day of Christ I will have reason to glory because I did not run in vain nor toil in vain. But even if I am being poured out as a drink offering upon the sacrifice and service of your faith, I rejoice and share my joy with you all. You too, I urge you, rejoice in the same way and share your joy with me. (Phil. 2:16–18)

Remember, Paul doesn't even know at this point if he is going to live or die. He is awaiting trial, and the resolution of his case is still very much up in the air. But even if he is going to be executed—even if he is being poured out as a drink offering on the altar of sacrifice for their benefit and God's glory—the love, unity, humility, and shining testimony of this church is a cause for rejoicing.

Paul has made it clear from the beginning of this letter (chapter 1) that he is choosing joy. It would be easy in his circumstances to think negatively, but he knows that God is writing a much larger story than his natural eyes can see at ground level. He is convinced that God is working out everything for good. He has seen God at work again and again in his adversity, even when he first came to Philippi and was beaten, jailed, and then miraculously delivered. He maintained joy even in that painful situation, and he continues to rejoice in everything.

Joy was the calling card of the early church in the midst of incredibly difficult circumstances. No one would have been impressed by whining or blaming, but many people were drawn to Christ because of the faith, endurance, and joy of Christians who were being marginalized, oppressed, and persecuted. Joy in those kinds of circumstances is either delusional or rooted in a greater reality, and for early believers, it was rooted in their relationship with Jesus and His promise of eternal life. In the here and now, life was very unfair. In the vast landscape of eternity, their troubles were light and momentary. They understood that the worst that can happen to a believer in this life is to die—and the best is to be with Jesus in glory forever.

The evidence of Jesus within them changed the world.

That's why Paul rejoiced, and why he encouraged the Philippians to shine like stars, no matter how dark the night became. And historically, from them and many other ancient believers, we know they did because the church grew. The evidence of Jesus within them changed the world. They had joy despite super challenging circumstances, and choose love for each other regardless of their differences, and even love for their enemies.

SHINING BRIGHTER

Paul called the Philippians to a high standard—living above reproach—and if we aren't careful, we can get the impression that we are failing on every front. After all, we don't always have our tongues tamed, we aren't always blameless in our testimony to the world, and we don't always shine as brightly as we could. Never forget that we are works in progress.

We can be encouraged that God doesn't make us put a quarter in the jar every time something negative slips out of our mouths. Otherwise many of us would be living in poverty. Or He doesn't set us aside every time we judge another person harshly because of their political opinions or personal biases. Otherwise we'd have no hope of unity within our fellowship or a good reputation outside of it. But He does keep calling us higher.

God is always renewing. He is doing great things in His people individually and as a body. It begins with our commitments, even small ones, like deciding to get control of our words or finding accountability partners to help us live differently. When individual lives change, families change, churches change, and communities change. Small points of light grow into bright, shining stars.

What have you expected from God, and what does He expect of you? In what ways are you partnering with Him to work out what

He has worked into you? How are you mining your salvation for all the riches it contains? And how are you living as a light in this darkened world? You may not be able to answer these questions fully at any given moment, but if you ask them of yourself daily and seek to answer them in all you do, you'll find yourself growing into the likeness of Jesus.

Choose one or two things to work on—attitude, authenticity, speech, godliness, boldness—and go into training, preferably with some friends who love you. Start taking note of your progress. It will build your faith because you will see God at work within you. You'll be encouraged to know that you are part of a grand scheme of the eternal God who is reconciling all things to Himself. One day when you bow your knee to Jesus, along with everyone else in the universe, it will be in glorious worship after a challenging but hope-filled journey. But it begins with small steps of *obedience*.

QUESTIONS FOR REFLECTION/DISCUSSION

1. Where do you see growth and progress in "working out" what God has "worked in" your life? List three or four things that God has done in your life that weren't true before you came to know Christ.

2. Where do you need to focus your effort and energy to allow Jesus' life to be manifested "in" and "through" you?

- Your Attitude? Become more grateful and positive
- Your Speech? Hold others up?
- Your Godliness? Deal with a moral issue /sexual purity?
- Your Authenticity? Be more real with what's going on inside you.
- Your Boldness? Refuse to be intimidated and openly identify with Jesus.

3. Check one or two of the above and share what next steps would help you grow and/or what help you might need from others.

Part 4: Love Cares

Then the righteous will answer him, "Lord,
when did we see you hungry and feed you, or
thirsty and give you something to drink?
When did we see you a stranger and invite you
in, or needing clothes and clothe you?
When did we see you sick or in prison and go to
visit you?"
The King will reply, "Truly I tell you, whatever you
did for one of the least of these brothers and
sisters of mine,
you did for me."

Matthew 25:37–40 NIV

CHAPTER 7

Love Cares

Theresa has an interesting habit. She calls it shopping. I call it searching.

She doesn't shop for herself very often, but we have twelve grandchildren, and those grandchildren have eight parents among them. It seems like we have a birthday in our family almost every week. So, Theresa is almost always searching for a gift to get somebody. Even in July, she's thinking about who would like what for Christmas.

She's great at it. She has eyes for it, always looking for something special for everyone in our family. She wants everyone to have just the right gift.

God is like that. He's searching all the time too—for people, not gifts for special occasions. In fact, searching is one of His lesser-known characteristics. He isn't necessarily looking for the smartest or most gifted people, though. He is looking for the kind of person He can trust to bring His light and love into a fallen and hurting world. He wants to support people who offer His forgiveness and restoration.

In one of the best-known passages of the New Testament, Jesus told Nicodemus that God loved the world so much that He gave His only Son so that whoever believes in Him will not perish but have everlasting life (John 3:16). In the next few verses, Jesus explained that He did not come to condemn the world but to save it—to offer life, love, and forgiveness. Peter later reiterated the same point—that God doesn't want anyone to perish but for all to come to repentance (2 Peter 3:9). So if God is looking for people who share His heart and carry His message, they will be the kind of people who embody these truths. He is searching for people who love Him and love others well. It's no doubt hard, but God is looking for people who *really care.*

WHY DOES GOD USE SOME PEOPLE AND NOT OTHERS?

Jesus told His followers that they would be the salt of the earth and light of the world (Matt. 5:13–14). They will flavor and brighten this world. But that doesn't mean He is looking for people who know how to shine or have a natural brilliance to them. They don't have to be famous or do anything noteworthy in the eyes of others. In fact, He is usually looking for the opposite: very ordinary people who will shine wherever they already are.

This can be hard to grasp for those of us who are so steeped in celebrity culture. We look to people with big names and huge followings. Even ordinary people who become "influencers" are soon treated as extraordinary. But there are no Christian superstars, a point emphasized repeatedly by people who understand what the Holy Spirit can do in anyone's life.[4] Spiritually speaking, no one is big or small. We are only consecrated or unconsecrated, surrendered to God or not. Some people may be more or less visible, depending on the gifts and the role God has given them. But before His throne, we will see remarkably faithful people whose names we never knew but who were powerfully used by God. Their hearts were right toward Him.

When God finds people like that, He helps them. He gives them opportunities, wisdom, courage, and whatever else they need to reflect His light into the world around them. Very often, it's someone completely ordinary and unexpected who would not have stood out from a human perspective. Gideon, for example, was fearfully threshing wheat in hiding when God called him to deliver Israel from the Midianites. David was the youngest of his brothers and the least likely to be anointed as the next king when God chose him for the throne. Jesus' disciples were not the up-and-coming leaders of their day when Jesus called them and eventually sent them out to change the world. But God sees into human hearts (1 Sam. 16:7). He knows how they will respond to Him, and strongly supports those who will align themselves with His love and forgiveness.

"I searched for a man among them who would build up the wall and stand in the gap before Me for the land, so that I would not destroy it; but I found no one."

We get occasional glimpses in Scripture of God looking for someone but not finding anyone whose heart is prepared for what He wants to do. I had a passion to memorize a lot of Scripture verses when I was young in the faith. I didn't always do it for the right reasons, but God used it to plant a lot of truth in my heart that has changed my life and stuck with me to this day. I came across one passage that I decided to memorize just because I thought it was so interesting. God had sent prophet after prophet to His people because He cared for them and wanted to forgive and restore them, yet this is what he told Ezekiel: "I searched for a man among them who would build up the wall and stand in the gap before Me for the land, so that I would not destroy it; but I found no one" (Ezek. 22:30). God wanted a representative to accomplish His purposes because He did not want to destroy His people. Tragically, no one had the right heart, so God poured out His judgment on them.

> "I searched for a man among them who would build up the wall and stand in the gap before Me for the land, so that I would not destroy it; but I found no one"

That's one of those mysteries involving God's sovereignty and human responsibility, and I'm not sure how it all works. But I remember thinking as a young Christian that standing in the gap is a huge responsibility for a person to carry. You stand in the gap for people wherever they are in their life so they can see God's light and love, and if you don't, they may never hear. That's a sobering thought.

A similar passage involving King Asa also shows God searching for someone He can support. After Solomon's death, Israel and Judah had a long history of unfaithful kings who did not please God, but occasionally one in Judah would honor Him. Asa was one of the good kings for much of his reign. He pulled down idols and shrines, confronted the idolatry in his own family, tried to reestablish worship of God in his kingdom, and trusted God as he fought valiantly against huge armies. Asa ruled faithfully for thirty years, and God blessed him with miracles, wealth, influence, and security.

But those blessings can often lead to complacency and self-sufficiency, and when the next wave of opposition came, Asa did not depend on God to defend him. Instead, he made an alliance with the king of Aram, a political enemy, to help Judah defeat Israel.

God was not pleased and sent a prophet named Hanani to deliver a message to Asa. God had wanted Asa to defeat the Arameans, not partner with them. Hanani reminded Asa that God had delivered him from powerful enemies in the past, so why wouldn't the king rely on God now? "For the eyes of the Lord move to and fro throughout the earth that He may strongly support those whose heart is completely His. You have acted foolishly in this. Indeed, from now on you will surely have wars" (2 Chron. 16:9).

For the eyes of the Lord move to and fro throughout the earth that He may strongly support those whose heart is completely His.

God judged Asa in this passage, but He judged him by proclaiming an amazing truth. This is an axiomatic principle regarding God's ways—that He is looking to save, restore, and bless. In fact, His eyes are surveying the entire globe, up and down the aisles of humanity, searching to and fro for people whose hearts are fully His. Why? Because He is eager to put the weight of His support behind them.

Can you imagine what that would be like—to have God's full support strengthening and carrying you? You don't have to imagine because this is God's promise to those who don't hold back in their love for Him and loyalty to His purposes. That's what "whose hearts are fully His" means.

I've gotten to know many venture capitalists over the years, and I've asked them what they look for when they are deciding whether to invest tens of millions of dollars in a great idea. One of them said, "The first thing I look for is something that can make a huge difference. We're always swinging for the fences. The next thing I look for is hunger in the person who is bringing the idea to us. They're passionate, teachable, and have an unusual sense of urgency, and they are willing to pay any price. Then, we look for character—people who won't give up, no matter what. And finally, we want people who can see the world going in one direction but have the foresight and creativity to see how it could be going in another direction." In other words, they are looking for people who are all in and willing to pursue their goals with zeal, persistence, and innovation regardless of the cost of sacrifice.

Do you know who the greatest venture capitalist in the entire universe is? God. But unlike today's venture capitalists, He isn't looking for people with a strong résumé, which is why His Word is filled with ordinary people whose hearts are His. That's the single most important qualification. Someone who says to Him (and means it), "I'll do whatever You want me to do and go wherever You want me to go"—whether it's selling a house in order to help people in need, setting aside a personal dream that doesn't fit the direction He is leading, relocating to a place that is not very desirable to most people but very strategic for the kingdom, or any other example of being a living sacrifice for Him. It's people who *care* about God and His agenda more than anything else.

"I'll do whatever You want me to do and go wherever You want me to go."

When God finds people who are available for Him to tap them on the shoulder and position them for His purposes, He steps in with His full support: "Here's the key to making it happen. Here are the resources. Here are the open doors and the people you need to go with you." When you go all in with Him, He goes all in with you.

BECOMING THAT PERSON

We've seen how love *gives, serves,* and *obeys*. In these last two chapters, we will see how love *cares*. Paul is nearing the end of this section of Philippians—the latter part of chapter 2—and expresses his *care* and concern for this church and gives them two examples of what care and concern look like. But in sharing these two examples, he also communicates a powerful message about the kind of person God is looking for. If we want to become someone God will strongly support, this section of Philippians shows us how.

The context for this passage, as we discovered earlier, was a problem with unity in the church. Paul told them that the answer is love. They should not think too highly of themselves but consider each other's needs more important than their own, living in humility and other-centeredness—the "I am second" approach to life. That's how love gives.

In verses 5–11, he gave them the ultimate example: Jesus, who did not cling to His deity, but humbled Himself by becoming like a bondservant, sacrificed His life for us, and then was highly exalted. The attitude of Jesus is the attitude we should have ourselves. That's how love serves.

Then in verses 12–18, Paul gave them a command to do all things without complaining or arguing to enhance their testimony among unbelievers and become shining lights in a dark world—to be grateful, godly, bold, and joyful servants who make a difference in their society by demonstrating the character of Jesus and the reality of eternity. That's how love obeys.

Now Paul presents models of how love *cares*. Not only does Paul care for these Philippian believers, as he has expressed throughout his letter. So does Timothy, his coworker, and Epaphroditus, the messenger they had sent to Paul in Rome. In carrying out their God-given assignments, each of these examples demonstrates the kind of care and concern we can all bring into every relationship. And in doing so, they show themselves to be the kind of person God will strongly support.

"Care about people" is a pretty basic message, isn't it? It doesn't seem very deep or complicated. Yet it's hard to imagine a message that is more needed in our world today. For one thing, many people don't show an ounce of concern for anyone else. Some have grown up as the center of attention and become entitled, while others struggled to look at themselves; both can lead to becoming incredibly self-centered. But even genuinely compassionate people can fall into the traps created by our self-focused society. We don't mean to be uncaring, but we live busy lives, get distracted by long to-do lists, are spread thin in our wide but not very deep social networks, and become preoccupied with our own concerns. We may care for our families and the needs right in front of us, but we often live as people who don't have time to care for much else.

Paul models his love and care by introducing two colleagues who also love and care. The first is Timothy. Paul has just presented to his readers a huge calling to live as lights in the world, but he doesn't want them to think they are in this alone. He wants to help them by sending Timothy to them soon.

THE PURPOSE FOR SENDING TIMOTHY: PAUL CARES

Paul's tenderheartedness toward these believers is apparent throughout this letter, and here it shows up in his desire to connect with them again: "But I hope in the Lord Jesus to send Timothy to you shortly, so that I also may be encouraged when I learn of your condition" (Phil. 2:19).

We may think of Paul as a visionary so preoccupied with big thoughts and a trailblazing mission that he shouldn't be distracted by minor concerns like the day-to-day functioning of a church or the emotional condition of its members. He was a highly educated Jew and Roman citizen and wrote thirteen books of the New Testament, which profoundly shaped the early church and world history.

But Paul had a shepherd's heart. He *cared*. He remembered this church fondly, from those early days with Lydia and her household to the dramatic conversion of the jailer who was afraid for his life to the people who were on his heart as he sat in confinement in Rome. He had watched that young church grow and prayed for them with zeal and affection. When he heard through Epaphroditus that they were having some trouble, he prioritized their concerns over his own—which, in light of his possibly pending execution, were pretty substantial. And even though having Timothy by his side was probably an enormous help, Paul was willing to sacrifice by sending his righthand man to Philippi to support them.

Why? "So I might be encouraged," he says. Even though he was brilliant at theology and missions, always thinking big thoughts about God and eternal life, he knew he would be cheered up by knowing how his friends were doing.

THE REASON TIMOTHY IS CHOSEN: HE CARES

Paul's description of Timothy tells us a lot about this young coworker's heart:

> For I have no one else of kindred spirit who will genuinely be concerned for your welfare. For they all seek after their own interests, not those of Christ Jesus. But you know of his proven worth, that he served with me in the furtherance of the gospel like a child serving his father. Therefore I hope to send him immediately, as soon as I see how things go with me; and I trust in the Lord that I myself also will be coming shortly. (Phil. 2:20–24)

Paul knew and worked with a lot of people. He was the apostle to the Gentiles, a man through whom God had done countless miracles and birthed numerous churches, a leader among leaders in the Christian movement. Yet he surprisingly says he has no one else of kindred spirit other than Timothy.

Maybe Paul meant that he had no one else nearby, or that of all the people who shared Paul's heart for God and ministry, Timothy understood him the best. But earlier in this letter, Paul wrote of opponents and rivals, as well as sympathetic people who might have wondered why God sidelined Paul in prison for such a long time or who were simply discouraged by his imprisonment because they couldn't see what God was doing in it (Phil. 1:12–18, 29–30). Paul knew from experience that leadership is lonely. There were people who had once worked with him and then rejected his message, and Paul sometimes felt deserted (2 Tim. 4:9–18). Yet he knew Timothy as a faithful friend and likeminded coworker. Timothy cared the way Paul cared. They were in sync. So his first choice for sending someone to check up on the Philippians was this young man who would be "genuinely concerned for [their] welfare."

Sadly, Paul knew people who did not come even close to fitting that description. He wrote of those who sought after their own interests rather than those of Jesus (v. 21). Even committed Christians can lose perspective and have self-serving agendas.

We see the same problem today, don't we? And it usually isn't intentional. Managing and growing churches can easily slip into a pursuit of programs, numbers, platforms, media, and budgets. *How do we get more visibility? Are we attracting the right people? What can we do to grow our financial support?* These aren't bad questions, but neither are they the main focus. If we were running a business, they would be paramount. If we're reaching hearts and minds with the gospel of truth and love, they should serve our purpose, not become our purpose. But it is very tempting and very easy for the primary and secondary to switch places in churches as well as our personal lives.

It is a battle for all of us to live from a pure, simple devotion to Christ.

That may be one reason we've seen so many spiritual failures among leaders we've known and loved. In most cases, they aren't wolves in sheep's clothing. They aren't bad people or con artists. They are most often committed, devoted men and women who began to drift somewhere in the past, and little by little stepped into thoughts and behaviors that caused them to disqualify themselves from effective, Christ-honoring ministry. Some who have fallen have had great positive influence in my life and ministry. Others I knew well, friends I shared with, ministered with, and learned from. It is a battle for all of us to live from a pure, simple devotion to Christ. It's a vivid reminder that none of us are immune to the powerful pull of this world and the attacks of the Evil One.

Paul witnessed this kind of attrition in his circles too, and toward the end of his ministry seemed to feel that he had few around him with the right heart to do the right things for the right reasons. But Timothy was an exception. "You know of his proven worth," Paul wrote. The phrase literally means Timothy had been tested and proven true. He chose to *care*!

Not that Timothy was perfect. Again, God is looking for ordinary people. Timothy fit that description. Paul had met him on an earlier missionary journey. He came from a half-Jewish, half-Greek family, but his mother and grandmother were followers of Jesus. He also had some personality and health issues to overcome; Paul encouraged him not to be so timid and gave him some advice for dealing with his digestion and other ailments (1 Tim. 5:23; 2 Tim. 1:7). But Timothy was faithful, and that's what both God and Paul were looking for.

Timothy was a "kindred spirit" with Paul. The phrase literally means "equal souled." That's a great picture. His soul and Paul's connected with each other and with God over the same issues. It's challenging to find people who aren't trying to push their own agenda, but Timothy didn't have one of his own. His agenda was God's. And that's the kind of person God is able to use most effectively.

So Paul intended to send Timothy to Philippi "immediately, as soon as I see how things go with me"—in other words, as soon as Paul knew the outcome of his trial and therefore, potentially, the length of his remaining life. Even so, Paul had already expressed confidence that he would continue to live (1:25), and therefore hoped to come too. His heart was with them already. Paul chose to *care*!

You may not know many people who live with this kind of concern for others and go out of their way to connect—people who are there for you when nobody else has time. But they are out there, and I believe their reward will be great. When someone is going through a rough period, gets a terrifying diagnosis, is struggling through rehab, is trying to salvage a broken marriage or recover from one that has already ended, or desperately needs someone to walk them into a new or deeper relationship with Jesus, these people are just there. Others may clam up and avoid those situations, but these open their lives to the people around them. That's what caring looks like.

When Theresa was going through cancer treatments about fifteen years ago, some friends of ours from Monterey would drive an hour and a half around mountains and in bad traffic—the traffic is always bad on that route—to bring us food. I don't even remember what the food was, but I do remember how humbling it was for people to *care* enough to go that far out of their way to help. There's something that connects your heart with people when you and they care. We're still in touch even though they moved to the east coast. Real caring does something deep and lasting in a relationship.

If you know people like that who have really cared for you—who have been equal-souled with you in a time of need—consider sending them a note or calling them today with a "thank you." Communicating with people is one of the most important things we can do to show that we care. Love engages. It demonstrates by action that other people really matter. I think people who have shown that they care would be encouraged by hearing how much they mattered. Some may not even remember; humble, selfless, loving people often don't realize how impactful they have been. But they are worth affirming. And like a muscle that grows with use, our love grows when we develop the habit of caring—especially in the little things.

They are also worth imitating. This is the model Paul presents for us to follow. People who are kindred spirits, who are genuinely concerned, and who do not seek their own interests but those of Christ in order to serve, are people God powerfully uses.

THE REASON EPAPHRODITUS IS SENT: HE CARES

The story doesn't end with Paul and Timothy. It is clear that they care for the Philippians, but Paul also wants to highlight another example of caring. The man sent from Philippi to deliver the church's financial gift to Paul has fallen ill. He has selflessly served his own church and Paul, but his sacrifice has cost a lot.

> But I thought it necessary to send to you Epaphroditus, my brother and fellow worker and fellow soldier, who is also your messenger and minister to my need; because he was longing for you all and was distressed because you had heard that he was sick. For indeed he was sick to the point of death, but God had mercy on him, and not on him only but also on me, so that I would not have sorrow upon sorrow. Therefore I have sent him all the more eagerly so that when you see him again you may rejoice and I may be less concerned about you. Receive him then in the Lord with all joy, and hold men like him in high regard; because he came close to death for the work of Christ, risking his life to complete what was deficient in your service to me. (Phil. 2:25–30)

Notice Paul's description of this man who *cares*: "brother," "fellow worker," "fellow soldier," and "your messenger and minister." That's a great résumé. Epaphroditus had been sent from Philippi to Rome because he cared for Paul; now, in his sickness, he is concerned about his fellow Philippians because he knows his condition would distress them. Having recovered from the point of death, he is ready for Paul to send him back home.

We've covered some of Epaphroditus' back story, as well as the context for Paul's letter to the Philippians. Philippi was one of the few churches, perhaps the only one at times, to support Paul financially. The Philippians knew of Paul's imprisonment, and they knew that Roman prisoners living under house arrest were required to pay their own room and board. If a prisoner couldn't pay for food or didn't have friends who would bring it to him, then he wouldn't eat. Paul was blessed with visitors (Acts 28:30–31), some of whom surely brought him meals, and Timothy was there at least some of the time to help. But Paul had no way of earning a living. He could only receive support, and the Philippians wanted to give it to him.

So Epaphroditus came with financial aid and spent some time with Paul. He shared news of what was going on in Philippi—that's how Paul knew the situations he addressed in his letter—and Paul viewed him with love and affection, as we can tell from the emotional language he uses in this passage. Paul "eagerly" sent him back for their joy—a major theme of the letter—and to relieve his own concern. But he wanted these believers to hold Epaphroditus in high regard because he risked his life to serve Christ, and in serving Christ, to serve Paul. Here we are reminded that real caring is more than emotional concern or a kind word; caring—*real caring*—involves sacrifice.

THE POWER OF PICTURES

Timothy and Epaphroditus exemplify the kind of person God uses to fulfill His purposes on earth.

Paul began this chapter with a call for believers to humbly and sacrificially love each other, then followed with the ultimate example of how Jesus left heaven to serve and sacrifice His life on earth. It seems fitting that he would end this section with examples of the same kind of love, using people who were very familiar to the Philippians, as if to say, "You know how Jesus embodied love that gives, serves, obeys, and cares, but you've also seen it in Timothy and Epaphroditus." Timothy and Epaphroditus exemplify the kind of person God uses to fulfill His purposes on earth.

It's often said that truth is better caught than taught. Paul never hesitates to teach, but he also knows the power of a picture. Throughout this letter Paul gives plenty of pictures: Jesus, himself, and these two friends and coworkers among them.

One of my prayers is that God would continue to work in my life to the point that someone might describe me the way Paul described Timothy and Epaphroditus: a kindred spirit, genuinely concerned, servant-hearted, no agenda but God's, a brother, fellow worker, and fellow soldier. Wouldn't you like to be described that way? These are some of the highest compliments one servant of God can give another. This is what love that cares produces in our lives and relationships.

Having the characteristics Paul has described will lead to that kind of honor. Those who prioritize others over themselves . . . who have the attitude of Christ within them and follow His pattern of humble, sacrificial service . . . who live as bright lights in the midst of the darkness around them . . . who love in a way that *gives, serves, obeys,* and *cares* . . . these are the ones who experience God's full support because He has scanned the horizons of this world and found their hearts to be fully His.

Make that your highest goal. As God sovereignly works within you to accomplish His purposes, partner with Him to mine the riches of your salvation and become the shining light and sacrificial servant He holds in high esteem. Like Paul, Timothy, and Epaphroditus, *care* for others in love, just as God has cared for you. You don't have to wait to be loved, you can "choose to love" today by caring for those around you and experience God's powerful support.

QUESTIONS FOR REFLECTION/DISCUSSION

1. Can you remember a time when God used your life to help someone in a significant way? How did it feel?

2. Who has cared for you in a way that expressed God's love and concern for you? What do you think would be the best way to affirm or thank them?

3. Why do you think God sometimes passes over "talented and gifted" people to use people like Timothy?

4. It's great to care when we feel that warm desire to reach out; but Paul, Timothy, and Epaphroditus cared when it was difficult, inconvenient, and costly. Who needs your care this week that you'd rather not care about? How could you "choose love" even if you don't feel like it and/or it would require some form of personal cost?

CHAPTER 8

Four Things God Is Looking For

We saw in the previous chapter that God supports those whose hearts are fully His, and we saw examples of that kind of person as Paul described the loving care of Timothy and Epaphroditus. If God is searching for regular people like you and me in order to strongly support us and use us for His purposes, we need to know specifically what He is looking for.

Beyond loving and caring, what characteristics position us to be used powerfully by Him?

What does it mean to stand in the gap for our families, our neighborhoods, our schools, our workplaces, our churches, and our society?

What does it look like to depend on God's presence, provision, and power?

How can we know if we are aligning with His purposes?

There may be many characteristics or qualities God is looking for in the people He wants to use, but He highlights four key attributes through Paul's words in Philippians 2:19–30. It is clear from this passage that standing in the gap as a representative of God is not left for superstars or high-profile ministers to do. It's for each of us as we respond to God with baby steps of obedience to bring light, love, kindness, holiness, and truth into the world around us. Only hearts with these characteristics can step into a world of fear, bitterness, anger, deception, and corruption with the love, purity, and full support of God.

Standing in the gap as a representative of God is not left for superstars or high-profile ministers to do.

When God is searching for someone to fully support and use for His purposes—when He surveys His world to find men, women, students, couples, churches, ministries, or any other person or organization fully committed to Him—He looks for four specific attributes we can observe in this passage. As you seek to position yourself for His purposes, consider these four questions:

QUESTION 1: DO YOU HAVE A SERVANT'S HEART?

It should be clear by now that serving is a prerequisite for reflecting the character of Jesus. It has been one of the most prominent themes of this chapter of Philippians, and, of course, a key part of Jesus' mission during His ministry on earth: "Even the Son of Man did not come to be served, but to serve, and to give His life a ransom for many" (Mark 10:45). Paul presented Jesus' example as the centerpiece of his appeals to the Philippians to love and serve each other.

Remember our discussion of servanthood in chapter 4? A servant would say, "No job is too low and no credit or thanks is needed. No one needs to see, no one needs to affirm, no one needs to remember." We may like to be affirmed and thanked, and it's always appreciated, but a servant isn't put out by doing what he or she should do. God sees that kind of heart and is drawn to it. In Luke 17 Jesus makes this point for His disciples in no uncertain terms.

> "Which of you, having a slave plowing or tending sheep, will say to him when he has come in from the field, 'Come immediately and sit down to eat'? But will he not say to him, 'Prepare something for me to eat, and properly clothe yourself and serve me while I eat and drink; and afterward you may eat and drink'? He does not thank the slave because he did the things which were commanded, does he? So you too, when you do all the things which are commanded you, say, 'We are unworthy slaves; we have done only that which we ought to have done.'" (Luke 17:7–10)

When I think of what a servant's heart looks like in our day, Greg Kucala comes immediately to mind. Greg is a high-tech guy who left a really good job with lots of benefits to take over the tech area at our church in Santa Cruz twenty-five years ago. Later he became the chief of staff for our ministry. Every time I speak, Greg comes in to check on me ahead of time, see how things are going, and pray with me. I don't have any administrative gifts, so Greg has taken on various roles, done a lot of hiring and organizing, and managed a lot of areas that I'm not equipped to do. When I was called in 2002 to another ministry across the country, I asked him if he would pray about relocating his family and coming with us. He did. We've been through a lot of ups and downs, and he's not only my colleague but also my friend. He has a servant's heart and has voluntarily changed roles at Living on the Edge and demoted himself organizationally when he felt someone else was a better fit than him. No job has been too big or too small. He makes everyone better and like oil in an engine, Greg serves in a way that carries the organization to run smoothly and effectively. I've seen God show up in his life again and again. That's the kind of heart God is looking for.

Closer to home, my wife Theresa has modeled a servant's heart that few ever see. I get looks of affirmation and compliments because my gifts are visible and public; but no one sees the hours my wife has prayed for me, the ministry, and the deep challenges we've faced as a family. She was willing to leave family in West Virginia to launch out with me to go to seminary in Texas. It was even harder for her when the next step meant leaving friends, uprooting four children, and making Santa Cruz our new home for twelve years. From there, it got even harder following the death of her mother as we moved to Atlanta. Theresa left our home, our church, her role as pastor's wife, and supported me and helped our daughter to adjust to a new life in Atlanta for seven years. With few exceptions, Theresa doesn't complain; she makes all of our lives work, mentors hurting women, manages the logistics of life with four grown children and twelve grandchildren, and is my best friend, wisest counselor, and encourager.

There was one more move that she emotionally could not come to terms with, and yet she said, "Chip, I absolutely don't want to go; but if you believe with all your heart this is God's will, I will follow." She modeled Luke 17 and I am humbled and challenged to follow her example.

One way to know if you have a servant's heart is to ask yourself how often you pray this prayer: *Lord, will You show me where to serve?* If you aren't asking God to give you opportunities to serve, start doing that now. He will gladly lead you into places of service that fulfill His purposes and satisfy your heart.

QUESTION #2: ARE YOU WILLING AND AVAILABLE?

I know a number of people who are *willing* to do anything God is leading them to do. I also know a number of people who are *available* to do anything God is leading them to do. But finding people who are both willing and available is much harder. Many are willing but unavailable; they have allowed their lives to get so full that they are limited in what they can do. Many are available but unwilling; they are so attached to their current situation that they can't envision God moving them into another. But those who are willing and available live with a readiness to respond to whatever God is saying.

A hurried, cluttered, busy lifestyle will kill love in relationships, including our relationship with God.

A hurried, cluttered, busy lifestyle will kill love in relationships, including our relationship with God. It fills our lives with "stuff," and the stuff takes center stage while love fades into the background. For this reason, I think that every believer should take stock of their life from time to time—take a huge step back, look at everything they are doing (jobs, ministries, practices, relationships) and think, *Does all of this still make sense?* We need to be able to discern the end of one season of life and ask God what the new one should look like, recalibrating our vision with our willingness and availability to love. When was the last time you did that?

Sometimes, for example, we don't need to make more money. Some people may be at a stage in life when they do, or perhaps want to make more money in order to give more. But striving for bigger,

We need to be open to change, but if you're a people-pleaser like me, change won't be easy.

better, and more doesn't always make sense. We miss God's best when we unnecessarily assume that we should just keep moving in the same direction as always.

The same could be said of our schedules. Are we filling them with busyness that keeps us from being available to God? What if He wants to redirect us? Would we be able to say yes? Sometimes we continue in the same patterns because we're used to them, not because they make sense for us now. Again, pushing the pause button to reevaluate is crucial.

I have the privilege of working with a number of pastors here in the US and around the world. Many are frustrated and struggling because they're trying to perpetuate ministries that aren't fruitful, aren't their passion, and are keeping them from even thinking about other possibilities. I know businesspeople who do the same thing. Each of us has a short amount of time to invest our gifts where they count the most. There's no better time to do that than now.

Take inventory of the clutter in your life—literally and figuratively. Many of us have closets full of things we think we might need one day but never will. Most of us tend to fill our lives with so much, both materially and with activities, that we limit our options and remain stuck where we are. A willing and available servant is always asking, "Lord, is this role, this place, this ministry still Your plan?"

We need to be open to change, but if you're a people-pleaser like me, change won't be easy. It will require saying no to some people. Believe it or not, that isn't necessarily a bad thing.

Many years ago, a godly businessman who loved and cared for me saw how I was struggling with everything on my plate. With kindness in his eyes and a Texas twang in his voice, he asked, "So you're indispensable?"

"No," I answered. *Not when you put it that way*, I thought.

"Well, you feel like you have to do everything, don't you?"

I wasn't sure what to say, but he was right. I did feel like I had to do everything myself. I was a young pastor in a small church and was bent on pleasing God and proving my worth. I did the preaching, led the music for a while, cut the grass, made all the hospital visits, led the elders' meetings, and was training a couple to take over the children's ministry in our little church of thirty-five members.

"Young man, I've got news for you. You'll find out sooner or later that your whole life is like a bucket of water. You stick your hand in that bucket and pull your hand out, and afterward it looks just the same." His point was that it all doesn't depend on me and if for whatever reason I was gone tomorrow, life would move on just fine without me.

> **If you're going to make significant changes and streamline your life, you'll need to eliminate something, not tweak it.**

This gentleman wasn't trying to minimize what I was doing. Our obedience and fruitfulness matter very much to God. But many of us are involved in a lot of things out of obligation or false responsibility, not obedience to what God has actually called us to do. We feel as if we'll let someone down or assume that only we can do what needs to be done. But if we are really going to love people and be the servant God wants us to be, we need to be focused. If we don't have time for God and for healthy relationships with others, we're too busy.

One of the greatest lessons I've learned is that you cannot tweak your way to change. We try to tweak our schedules, tweak our lifestyles, move a little in this or that direction, and try to make everything still fit. But I'll be honest with you: If you're going to make significant changes and streamline your life, you'll need to eliminate something, not tweak it. You decide you will no longer do that activity, serve on that committee, pursue that time-consuming habit, or cling to all that junk that just gets in the way.

When you take that step back and reevaluate, you may decide you're exactly where you need to be. That's great. Don't change just for the sake of change. But you may find that you need to make some adjustments, and God will honor your willingness to be available.

Sadly, some people don't serve because they don't think they have anything to give. There can be many reasons for that: a belief that they don't have any gifts or skills, shame regarding their past, negative experiences with other Christians (especially people in leadership), and more. But as we've seen, God uses "ordinary" people (although none of His people is ordinary in His eyes), and He also uses people who don't have anything close to a squeaky-clean record (like Moses the murderer, Rahab the prostitute, David the adulterer, Paul the persecutor, Matthew the traitorous tax collector). If you think you have to have it all together to serve Him, you've forgotten how He has worked through people throughout history and today. Regardless of your track record—things you have done or that have been done to you, whether it includes a divorce, bankruptcy, an abortion, abuse, a lot of burned bridges, or anything else—you have something to offer.

I grew up in a church that had a lot of stained-glass windows portraying the saintly lives of the apostles. I love stained glass, but as a kid, I didn't get the right message from the images it showed me. I read the Bible when I got older, and it changed everything.

One of the best things that ever happened to me was realizing that all of these "saintly" people were as messed up as I was, some much worse.

Our experiences of pain, dysfunction, trauma, and failure are highly valued in God's kingdom. When people showed up at our church carrying the pain of losing a loved one, an unwanted pregnancy, the loss of a friendship, ongoing illness, the loss of a job, unresolved bitterness, struggles with addiction, depression, loneliness, single parenthood, low self-esteem, or any other affliction common to humanity, we would pair them with someone in our congregation who had been through similar experiences. "Ordinary" people in our midst were qualified to serve, comfort, encourage, and strengthen others because of the baggage they once carried, and God used them powerfully. God uses people who will lay down their pride, be willing to get some training, and say, "I want God to use my brokenness and my pain to help others." He restores lives through people who have been or are being restored. You just have to be willing and available.

QUESTION #3: ARE YOU FAITHFUL IN THE ASSIGNMENTS GOD GIVES YOU?

Most Christians consider themselves faithful—generally. But when we start thinking about specifics—faithfulness to pray and read God's Word consistently, to fully invest in the relationships that are important to us, to steward our finances as diligently as we intended—we realize how much room we have to improve.

One proverb puts it like this: "Many claim to have unfailing love, but a faithful person who can find?" (Prov. 20:6 NIV). Jesus said that the way we handle finances reflects how we would handle greater things: "He who is faithful in a very little thing is faithful also in much; and he who is unrighteous in a very little thing is unrighteous also in much. Therefore if you have not been faithful in the use of unrighteous wealth, who will entrust the true riches to you?" (Luke 16:10–11). What we do with the assignments God has given us determines whether He will give us more.

Jesus talked a lot about finances for at least two reasons. First, what we do with money represents our values. Second, He's looking for faith, and we demonstrate faith (or lack of it) in how we handle money. People who are diligent to give the first portion of their income to God and then figure out how they can progressively give more and more are living by faith. When God sees that, He quite often entrusts us with more money; He also gives us greater spiritual responsibility, allowing us the amazing joy of leading people to Christ, helping them grow, and using our spiritual gifts for greater fruitfulness (Luke 16:10–14).

What we do with the assignments God has given us determines whether He will give us more.

Imagine having one employee who shows up every day and is diligent to do all of his work on time, and another who shows up late several times a week and never seems to finish the job. When you're looking for someone to handle greater responsibility, which one are you going to choose? Not a difficult question, is it? God is the same way.

People who have heard me speak or read my books are familiar with Dave Marshall, a bricklayer whom God used to changed my life. Dave wasn't flashy or cool, and his Bible studies weren't particularly dynamic or riveting. But he was faithful in the assignments God had given him. I had just come to Christ when I met him my first year in college, and I couldn't figure out whether I was really going to walk with God or keep hanging out in bars with the basketball team and doing things I knew I shouldn't do. Dave invited me into his home for dinner, met with me weekly (even when I blew our appointment off sometimes), and modeled what it meant to be a man. He cared. He wouldn't give up on me. He let me into his life so I could see what a Christian man looked like, how to parent your kids, and how to face adversity. The impact of Jesus in Dave's life made an impact on mine. And out of all the "great Christians" who have influenced my life, this ordinary Christian named Dave had the greatest impact. Until just a couple of years ago when God called Dave home, he was still working near a college campus and reaching out to students who need someone to care.

He let me into his life so I could see what a Christian man looked like.

So ask yourself if you've been faithful to the assignments God has given you—not if you've done them perfectly, but if you've approached them with the right heart and been diligent to fulfill them as well as you can. We never arrive at complete faithfulness, so perfection is not a helpful standard here. But are you progressing? Are you moving forward on your journey? This is how God uses people.

QUESTION #4: ARE YOU LOYAL AND TEACHABLE?

God is looking for people who are still growing and can be loyal over the long haul. That's essentially what Paul said about Timothy. He's tested and proven, he has a track record of loyal service, and he has the same genuine concern as Paul. He had spent years learning under Paul's mentorship.

When I first arrived at the church where I pastored for nine and a half years, I wasn't sure if we were going to make it. It was a great church in the late 1970s and early '80s, but had dwindled in attendance and had facilities in need of repair. We were millions of dollars in debt and bleeding thousands of dollars each week. We were an older white congregation in a multicultural neighborhood, and our mindset needed to change. The change was slow and hard. God raised up leaders and momentum grew as our vision to be a disciple-making church, not necessarily a big church, took hold. We rallied around Romans 12 discipleship, focused on our community, and saw God's favor poured out as the years passed. Thousands started attending and disciples were making disciples; then the floodgates opened with people from every ethnicity under the sun.

We were already translating the service into Korean and Mandarin, but we also needed people with kind hearts to pray for our non-English speakers after the service—and, when needed, help them find their way in whatever struggles they were facing. Jim started doing that. He was faithful, loyal, always there to help, like clockwork. And he always had a smile. Because of people like him, we continued to grow deep and wide. Then we had to figure out parking issues because it was a logjam. We were in desperate need for people to serve in the parking lot with a friendly smile and words of welcome, and Jim did that regularly too. He was always there, telling everyone, "Great to see you!" Hardly anyone knew that he and people like him is what turned that struggling church into a source of life in our community. Jim didn't have a high-profile position, but he did have a heart God could use.

God worked through Jim because he was servant-hearted, willing and available, and faithful in the assignments God had given him. And God blessed him too. He's one of our ministry partners to this day. He just keeps showing up where he's needed, and that's one of the secrets to being greatly used by God.

GROWING INTO OUR CALLING—TOGETHER

In the body of Christ, we get to be close to people whom God fully supports for being fully devoted to Him. I want to be more like those people. I want to be more like my wife, like Greg, like Jim, and like a lot of other people who may not be well known in the eyes of many around them but are very well known in heaven. The answer to the questions of whether they (1) have a servant's heart, (2) are willing and available, (3) are faithful in their assignments, and (4) are loyal and teachable is a resounding yes. They have what God is looking for.

If you're like most people, you may not be able to answer those four questions with a clear yes or no. You're probably servant-hearted, willing and available, faithful in the assignments God has given you, and loyal and teachable to some degree—not perfect in any of these areas, but not completely lacking either. As with most things in the Christian life, you have made progress and have lots of room to improve.

But don't let any ambiguity or uncertainty prevent you from wrestling with these questions seriously. As you look back on what God has already done in your life and look forward to what He wants to do, position yourself for maximum fruitfulness and fulfillment. It's very easy to drift away from the attitudes and responses God wants from us. No one wakes up one day and decides to be less loving, servant-hearted, or committed. It just sort of happens. So be intentional not only about holding your ground but advancing toward the high calling you've been given.

One way to do that is to get into a group that fosters an environment of mutual encouragement and accountability. We are called to stir one another up toward love and good deeds (Heb. 10:24). As iron sharpens iron, we sharpen one another in our relationship with God and each other (Prov. 27:17). Most of all, pray for each to choose love by giving, serving, obeying, and caring right where you are with the people God has placed in your life.

PUT IT INTO PRACTICE

As we wrap up our study of Philippians 2, I want to shift from teaching to coaching for a few minutes. Studies reveal that much of what we read in a book like this or listen to at an event is forgotten after about two or three days. No matter how much we absorb information as true and important, no matter how much we sense that God is working in our lives, it just doesn't stick with us and become our reality—*unless* we take some steps to work it deeper into our hearts and minds. So as we conclude, I want to provide some specific ways that have proven over the years to really help people grow:

Identify. First, set aside an hour or two to make a list of points in Philippians 2 where you sensed God speaking to you. If you underlined some sentences or made notes in the margins, you're already on your way to completing this step. But don't stop there. Make a list of things you think you need to work on, attitudes or actions you need to let go of, attitudes or actions you need to cultivate and more fully embrace, people you need to forgive or ask forgiveness from, commitments you need to reinforce, or any other points that resonated in your spirit as an area for change in your life.

Prioritize. Next, prioritize your list. Ask God to show you the top two or three items from the list to address first. Sit quietly with Him and let Him impress upon your heart the next steps He wants you to take. Don't try to do everything on your list at once; that becomes overwhelming very easily and causes people to burn out and give up after a couple of weeks. He will walk you through your transformation one step at a time. Change often happens like dominoes falling; topple one, and the rest are likely to follow. Just let Him speak to you about where to start.

Share. Find someone you trust—preferably of the same sex, though couples can work together on this too, depending on the issue—who loves you, cares for you, will be honest with you, and won't judge you or try to tell you what to do. Ask to get together for an hour or two and verbalize what God is teaching you. Share what steps you think you need to take and ask for feedback as well as accountability. *Am I on track? Does this sound like God's will? Do you have any experience with this?* Talking through what God is doing in your life has a way of reinforcing it and keeping it at the forefront of your mind.

This step is very important. It's often the difference between letting truth change your life and letting it pass through your mind without effect. Connect with someone who is willing to walk with you through your transformation process.

Let other people see transformation in you before you offer any suggestion that you think might be helpful for them.

Take the next step. After you get feedback, decide what step(s) God wants you to take. One of those steps may be asking the person you've talked to if he or she will help you keep your commitments to God. Ask if they are willing to set up a regular appointment—coffee together, a video call, whatever. You will likely not only be encouraged by this person's support but also find that they are inspired to do what you are doing too. Another step may be repairing a relationship, streamlining your life to be more available to God, or finding opportunities to serve. Let God lead you step by step as you implement what you have learned from His Word.

Be careful about trying to apply these truths to other people's lives. We often can see areas in other people's lives that need to change more easily than we can see them in ourselves. You know the plank in our eyes and the speck in theirs that Jesus warned about (Matt. 7:5)? There may be a time to have an honest conversation with a loved one about being more servant-hearted or selfless, but start with yourself. Let other people see transformation in you before you offer any suggestion that you think might be helpful for them. People are much more willing to own their issues when they know we are owning ours. If you do get to that point, be extremely tender in sharing anything that might cause them to feel misunderstood or defensive. Then be extremely gracious in hearing their heart.

Be wise and gentle with all of your next steps, with yourself and others.

Remember always that love endures forever. As Paul wrote in 1 Corinthians, faith, hope, and love abide, but the greatest of these is love. One day, we will not need faith, and our hope will be fulfilled. But love never ends. Pursuing love as a follower of Jesus is always a worthwhile goal. You never have to wonder if praying to love others well is God's will. He will always answer that prayer because love aligns us with His nature and fulfills His highest commandment. So ask Him daily, even hourly, to fill your life with His love and give you the wisdom and humility to love others well. He will produce in you the life and love of Jesus Himself.

QUESTIONS FOR REFLECTION/DISCUSSION

1. Rate yourself on a scale from 1–5 on the questions below of the Four Things God Is Looking For, where 1=Does not describe me at all and 5=That is absolutely true of me.

a. Do you have a servant's heart?
b. Are you willing and available?
c. Are you faithful in the assignments God gives you?
d. Are you loyal and teachable?

Evaluate: A rating of 1 or 2 signifies your highest priority of need to develop; ratings of 4–5 demonstrates you're making good progress. Avoid rating a 3 as it can be a "cop out" that reinforces the status quo or unwillingness to honestly assess your obedience/relationship to God.

2. What specifically do you need to stop or start doing to become the kind of person God can really use?

3. Who specifically could you call, meet with, or video conference to share your next steps? When will you do it?

Notes

1. Mark R. McMinn, "What Brilliant Psychologists Like Me Are Learning About Humility," *Christianity Today*, July/August 2017, https://www.christianitytoday.com/2017/06/what-brilliant-psychologists-humility/.
2. Arnold A. Dallimore, *George Whitefield: The Life and Times of the Great Evangelist of the Eighteenth-Century Revival* (Banner of Truth, 1970).
3. "Over Half of Practicing Christians Admit They Use Pornography," Barna, October 17, 2024, https://www.barna.com/trends/over-half-of-practicing-christians-admit-they-use-pornography/; https://www.barna.com/research/pastors-pornography-use/.
4. One of the best examples is a collection of messages by Francis Schaeffer in *No Little People* (InterVarsity Press, 1974).

Bibliography

Barclay, William. *The Letters to the Philippians, Colossians, and Thessalonians, Revised Edition*. Louisville, KY: The Westminster Press, 1975.

Gaebelein, Frank E. *The Expositor's Bible Commentary with The New International Version of The Holy Bible, Vol. 11*. Grand Rapids, MI: Zondervan Publishing House of The Zondervan Corporation, 1978.

Martin, Ralph P. *The Epistle of Paul to the Philippians: An Introduction and Commentary.* Grand Rapids, MI: William. B. Eerdmans Publishing Company, 1987.

Meyer, F. B. *Devotional Commentary on Philippians.* Grand Rapids, MI: Kregel Publications, 1979.

Phillips, J. B. *The New Testament in Modern English.* New York: The MacMillan Company, 1962.

Robertson, Archibald Thomas. *Word Pictures in the New Testament, Volume IV, The Epistles of Paul.* Nashville, TN: Broadman Press, 1931.

Ryrie, Charles Caldwell. *The Ryrie Study Bible New Testament, New American Standard Version.* Chicago: Moody Press, 1976.

Wiersbe, Warren W. *The Bible Exposition Commentary, Vol. 2.* Victor Books, 1989.

Wuest, Kenneth S. *The New Testament: An Expanded Translation*. Grand Rapids, MI: William B. Eerdmans Publishing Company, 1961.

Wuest, Kenneth S. *Wuest's Word Studies: From the Greek New Testament, Vol. II*. Grand Rapids, MI: William. B. Eerdmans Publishing Company, 1973.

I CHOOSE PEACE
I CHOOSE JOY
I CHOOSE LOVE
I CHOOSE
LOVE
HOW TO LOVE YOUR
NEIGHBOR AS YOURSELF
CHIPINGRAM
MOODY